THE OAKWOOD LIBRARY OF

# THE ST HELENS RAILWAY

## ITS RIVALS AND SUCCESSORS

*J M Tolson*

THE OAKWOOD PRESS
1983

ISBN 0 85361 292 7

*To my wife, Joan*

## CONTENTS

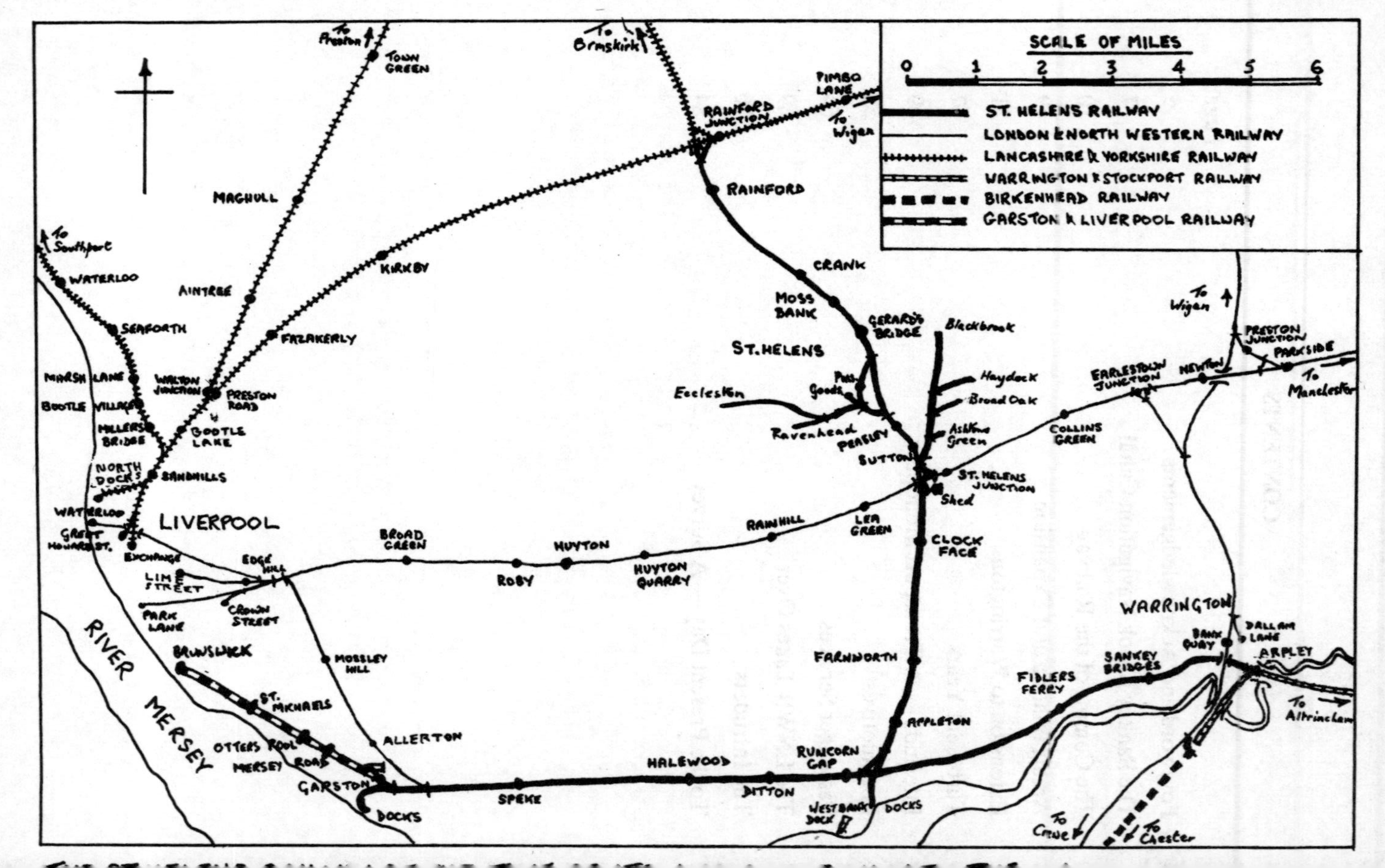
SCALE OF MILES
0 1 2 3 4 5 6
ST. HELENS RAILWAY
LONDON & NORTH WESTERN RAILWAY
LANCASHIRE & YORKSHIRE RAILWAY
WARRINGTON & STOCKPORT RAILWAY
BIRKENHEAD RAILWAY
GARSTON & LIVERPOOL RAILWAY
To Preston
TOWN GREEN
To Ormskirk
PIMBO LANE
RAINFORD JUNCTION
To Wigan
MAGHULL
RAINFORD
To Southport
WATERLOO
AINTREE
KIRKBY
CRANK
MOSS BANK
SEAFORTH
FAZAKERLY
GERARD'S BRIDGE
Blackbrook
ST. HELENS
To Wigan
PRESTON JUNCTION
PARKSIDE
MARSH LANE
WALTON JUNCTION
PRESTON ROAD
Pass.
Goods
Eccleston
Haydock
EARLESTOWN JUNCTION
NEWTON
To Manchester
BOOTLE
VILLAGE
Broad Oak
MILLERS BRIDGE
BOOTLE LANE
Ravenhead
PEASLEY
Ashton's Green
COLLINS GREEN
NORTH DOCKS
SANDHILLS
SUTTON
ST. HELENS JUNCTION
Shed
WATERLOO
LIVERPOOL
LEA GREEN
GREAT HOWARD ST.
RAINHILL
EXCHANGE
BROAD GREEN
HUYTON
CLOCK FACE
EDGE HILL
LIME STREET
ROBY
HUYTON QUARRY
PARK LANE
CROWN STREET
WARRINGTON
DALLAM LANE
BANK QUAY
RIVER MERSEY
BRUNSWICK
MOSSLEY HILL
FARNWORTH
ARPLEY
SANKEY BRIDGES
FIDLERS FERRY
ST. MICHAELS
To Altrincham
APPLETON
ALLERTON
OTTERS POOL
MERSEY ROAD
HALEWOOD
RUNCORN GAP
GARSTON
SPEKE
DITTON
DOCKS
WEST BANK DOCK
DOCKS
To Crewe
To Chester

# FOREWORD AND ACKNOWLEDGEMENTS

This short study has been condensed from a much longer unpublished work, in order to commemorate the 150th anniversary of the opening of the St Helens Railway main line in February 1833. The main sources of the narrative are the minute books of the St Helens & Runcorn Gap Railway (1830-44) and of the St Helens Canal & Railway (1845-1864). There is a considerable gap in these, from 19 March 1844 until 22 July 1845, while the amalgamation of canal and railway was being finalised, and the same lack of information also typified the last few months before the amalgamation with the LNWR. Parliamentary papers, minute books of other railways and contemporary newspaper reports have also been extensively consulted, together with a large number of published works on the various railways mentioned in the text.

In placing the St Helens Railway in the context of the developing industry of the area, the classic study of T C Barker and J R Harris 'A Merseyside Town in the Industrial Revolution — St Helens 1750-1900' has been invaluable both in its content and stimulus to further study. The more specific articles on the Sankey Brook Navigation by Professor Barker have also added to the author's knowledge, as no minute books of that waterway appear to have survived.

The chapter dealing with locomotive history has perhaps provided the greatest problems, because of the relatively scanty and often contradictory information available. Mr E Craven, a noted expert in early locomotive history, has given unstintingly of his time and knowledge to unravel the mysteries, and without his help it is unlikely that this chapter could have been written. Others who have helped with this chapter are R Currie, A G Dunbar, H Jack and the late G H Platt. Nevertheless any errors of fact or inference, particularly in the compilation of the appendices dealing with the locomotives, are solely the responsibility of the author; any corrections or additional information would be most welcome.

It is difficult to pay tribute to all those who have helped with the general preparation of this history over many years, but special mention must be made of the staff of the BRB Archives at Porchester Road, the County Records Office at Preston, and the staff of the libraries at Liverpool, Warrington and Widnes. However, the brunt of my researches has been borne by several reference librarians at St Helens Central Library and in particular Roger Hart, the current Administrative Officer. Others who have helped in a variety of ways, and to whom I acknowledge my debt are A Barlow, C Balstone, C R

Clinker, J Crompton, A C Gilbert, G O Holt, A E Kersey, N R Knight, J Marshall, C G Maggs, A W Neal, E J Norris, J Peden, B Reed, J M Ryan, F D Smith, C R Gordon Stuart and K H Vignoles.

My greatest indebtedness is however to my wife, Joan, who has typed several versions of the manuscript and encouraged me throughout this study.

*November 1982* JMT

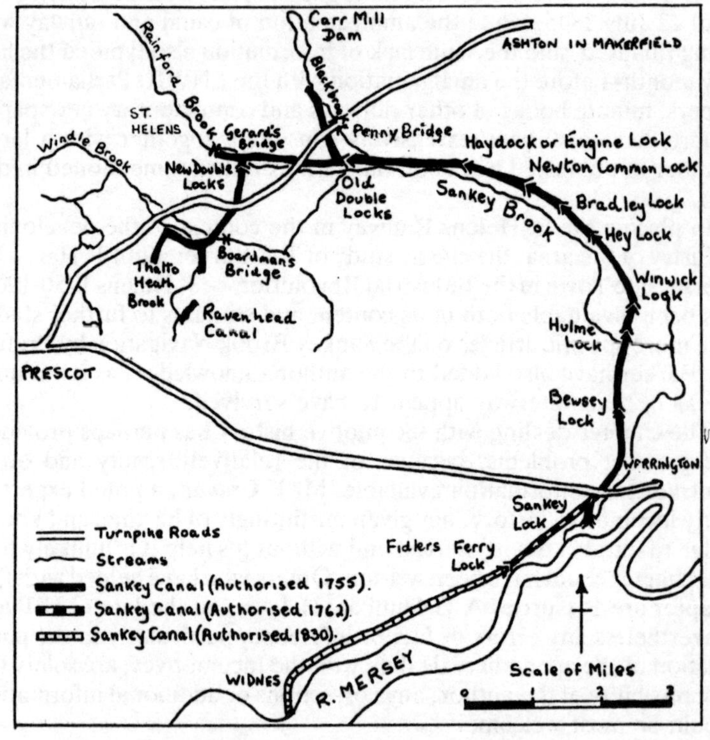


THE SANKEY BROOK NAVIGATION CANAL.

Showing main feeder streams and turnpike roads.

## CHAPTER I

# THE SANKEY BROOK NAVIGATION CANAL

The town of St Helens is known today as one of the foremost glass-producing centres in the world, with about one fifth of its 100,000 inhabitants engaged in that activity. Like many other Lancashire towns, it has been scarred by the industrial life of the last two centuries, as evidenced by the remains of pit-head winding gear, spoil heaps and residues from a variety of industries. In the early eighteenth century, however, the inhabitants of the area were mainly farmers or craftsmen, although even then a few glass blowers were to be found among them.

Primitive collieries in the shape of drift mines or shallow pits were already dotted about the landscape, and these were soon developed to supply the growing needs of the Cheshire saltfields, well before major coal-burning furnace industries were established in St Helens itself. Within twenty years of the opening of the Weaver Navigation in 1732, the tonnage of coal shipped up that waterway more than trebled, while the requirements of the growing port of Liverpool also meant that the rich and largely untapped coal deposits around St Helens were needed to supplement those in the Whiston and Prescot areas. Authority to extend the turnpike road from Prescot to St Helens, and then on to Ashton in Makerfield, was obtained in 1746 and 1753 respectively, but increases in tolls, and in the price of coal from the Prescot area, spurred on the Common Council (or Corporation) of Liverpool to investigate the use of water transport from St Helens to the River Mersey, and thence to Liverpool, in an effort to reduce fuel costs.

So in June 1754 two surveyors, Henry Berry and William Taylor, were engaged to examine the possibility of making navigable a small stream known as the Sankey Brook. This meandered in a circuitous course from St Helens to Warrington, and then ran back westwards to join the Mersey to the west of Sankey Bridges. In fact, the first 1¼ miles from the river up to Sankey Bridges had already been made navigable for boats of up to 60 tons burthen, and wharves and warehouses had been constructed there. The results of the survey were favourable, and with support from a variety of interested parties, it was decided to apply for Parliamentary sanction to make the Sankey Brook navigable up to St Helens. As there was no significant opposition to the Sankey Brook Navigation Bill, it had a relatively easy time in Parliament, and received the Royal Assent on 20 March 1755.

No limit was placed on the scheme's capital powers, and its promoters advertised 120 shares with a paid-up value of £155 each. Because of the speed with which the work was carried out, £90 was called for before the end of 1757, and the whole £18,600 was subscribed within eight years.

Although the Act had empowered the promoters "to make such new Cuts, Canals, Trenches or Passages for Water, in, upon or through the Lands or Grounds joining or near unto the same River [Sankey Brook] . . ., as they shall think proper and requisite", it was assumed that the normal procedure of dredging and widening the stream would be carried out, with cuts made only to eliminate awkward bends, and locks installed to control the water level. But Berry, a native of the area, knew the problems associated with the Sankey Brook, and with the support of the major shareholder, John Ashton, decided to cut a completely new waterway using the existing brook merely as a reservoir. Work began on 5 September 1755, and the canal joined the already navigable portion of the Sankey Brook via a lock a little below Sankey Bridges, and thereafter only crossed it at one point, near Hulme Lock, just over two miles away. In its eight mile course, the canal was raised through 80ft by eight single locks, and a staircase pair known as "Old Double Lock", the first of its kind in England. This was at Parr, where the waterway divided into two arms, the northerly branch, 800 yards in length, running to Penny Bridge at Blackbrook, while the main line continued westward for a further 1¼ miles to Gerard's Bridge in St Helens. On 4 November 1757 an advertisement in the 'Liverpool Chronicle' announced that the "Sankey Brook Navigation is now open for the passage of flats to the Haydock and Par Collierys". Work continued at the northern end, and by 1759 the waterway was substantially complete, some two years before the Duke of Bridgewater's canal from Worsley to Stretford, which is often considered as the first English canal.

On 8 April 1762, sanction was obtained to extend the two northern arms of the waterway by a further 1,200 yards, and also to provide an extension at the southern end from Sankey Lock to Fidlers Ferry, where a new entrance lock would improve access to the waterway. Although the southern extension was built relatively quickly, the northern extension to Blackbrook was not completed until about 1770. The main line was also extended to Boardman's Bridge past a second staircase pair at the junction with the Gerard's Bridge branch, whence in due course it reached newly founded copper and glass works, as well as at least one of the existing collieries. When completed about 1772, the waterway was some twelve miles in length and able to accept boats of up to 50 ton burthen. Its construction was notable for the use of swing bridges instead of the more usual fixed hump-back bridges, so that canal boats or "flats" could travel under sail, although towing by horses was more usual. To complement the waterway a network of colliery tramways was gradually built, the most famous of which was perhaps Sir Thomas Gerard's waggonway, which ran for some two miles from Pewfall Colliery near Garswood to Blackbrook Lower Wharf.

The 1755 Act had been explicit in setting the maximum toll at 10d per ton, and specified "that sixty three cubical Feet of Coal, Cannel Coal, Charcoal, Coke and Cinders, shall be deemed, rated and estimated a ton; and that Fifty Cubical Feet of Fir, Poplar, Withy or Willow and Forty Cubical feet of Oak, Ash, or any other Timber, shall be deemed, rated and estimated a Ton."

For coal this gave 27 or 28 cwt to the ton, although the so-called 'long' ton was more usually of 30 cwt. When coupled with the 'imperial' ton of 20 cwt, the variety of measurements gave plenty of scope for canal and railway to manipulate to their own advantage in the years to come. As many items such as "Limestone, Paving Stones, Gravel, Sand, Soapers Waste, Dung and all kinds of Manure" were free from tolls, it may seem surprising that the canal proprietors ever reaped any benefit from their investment. Yet the Sankey Brook Navigation, which declared its first dividend in April 1761, was to be a particularly profitable undertaking, and reputedly paid an average annual dividend of 33⅓%, until this was drastically reduced by railway competition. The 1762 Act provided for an additional 2d toll for craft using the extension from Fidlers Ferry, where it was claimed that the new entrance was still not wholly satisfactory.

Although the extension to Runcorn of the Duke of Bridgewater's Canal in 1776 and the Mersey & Irwell Navigation in 1804, caused the proprietors some concern, the overall trend was one of increasing utilisation and prosperity despite changes in the patterns of trade. In 1771 the Sankey Brook Navigation carried 89,720 tons, of which no less than 45,568 went to Liverpool, and a further 30,000 up the Weaver to the saltfields. But St Helens was about to develop its own industries, and in 1786 the huge Ravenhead works of the British Cast Plate Glass Manufacturers began production, to be followed four years later by the Ravenhead Copper Smelting Works. Within two years the latter works alone was consuming 700 tons of coal per week, all from an increasing number of local pits. Although the copper smelters were closed by 1815 because of a deep recession, the glass industry continued to flourish and provide increasing employment and trade for the canal, whose traffic was to grow from 17,600 tons a year in 1759 to 186,000 tons a year in 1820. Sankey Navigation shares, on the rare occasions they came on the market, could fetch up to eight times their nominal value. So, despite complaints about the inefficient way the waterway was run, and continuing demands for improvements in the access at Fidlers Ferry or for extensions towards Liverpool, the proprietors continued to benefit from industrial development in both St Helens and Liverpool, until well after the railway age had cast its dark shadow across the sunny horizon of the canal monopoly.

## CHAPTER II
# THE COMING OF THE RAILWAY

By the 1820s, the general dissatisfaction with canals in the north-west had reached a new peak, for having gained a virtual monopoly of bulk transport, many proprietors made only minimal efforts to maintain an effective operation, confident that no other means of transport could readily supplant them. Delays in traffic were frequent, particularly in winter when the waterways were frozen, just at the time coal supplies were most sorely needed, while in summer they were often adversely affected by a lack of water. By this time Liverpool and Manchester were linked by the circuitous route of the Leeds & Liverpool Canal to the north, and the more direct southern routes of the Mersey & Irwell Navigation and the Duke of Bridgewater's Canal. Both the latter undertakings appear to have been reasonably efficient, if allowances were made for their more obvious limitations, not the least being the need to travel some eighteen miles from Liverpool up the windswept and tidal Mersey estuary before the canals were reached, a problem they shared with the Sankey Brook Navigation.

Various schemes were propounded for a railway between the two major towns of Lancashire, but it was not until the promoters of the Liverpool & Manchester issued their first prospectus on 29 October 1824 that the threat to the waterways became a reality. Nevertheless improvements to canals continued to be made, and until the early 1840s waterways still carried over 60 per cent of the freight traffic between Liverpool and Manchester. It was originally intended that the L & M line would pass virtually through the centre of the area now covered by the town of St Helens, but opposition from powerful local landowners, coupled with the errors in the survey made by George Stephenson, caused the first proposals to be rejected by Parliament in June 1825. Stephenson was replaced as engineer by George and John Rennie. Their chief surveyor was Charles Blacker Vignoles, later to become engineer of the St Helens & Runcorn Gap Railway. His main task was to survey a route to minimise the landowners' objections to the railway, which he achieved by producing a scheme virtually on an east-west axis. He acquitted himself well in the 1826 Committee examinations on the revised proposals, but the recall of Stephenson in the following July led to Vignoles' resignation in February 1827, after a series of disagreements with his new chief. The L & M Bill received the Royal Assent on 5 May 1826, but the construction of the line, including the triumphal crossing of the infamous Chat Moss, the Rainhill trials of 1829, and the ceremonial opening on 15 September 1830, are too well known to require repetition here.

*The St Helens and Runcorn Gap Railway is Born*

The opening of the L & M line brought little immediate benefit to St Helens, and had only minimal effect on the trade which passed down the Sankey to the Cheshire saltfields. So in 1829, a number of local industrialists requested Vignoles, who obviously knew the area reasonably well, to carry out a survey for a line starting from Cowley Hill Colliery, just north of St Helens, and running southwards to a dock on the River Mersey at Runcorn Gap, some nine miles distant. They stipulated that the dock must be capable of admitting vessels of

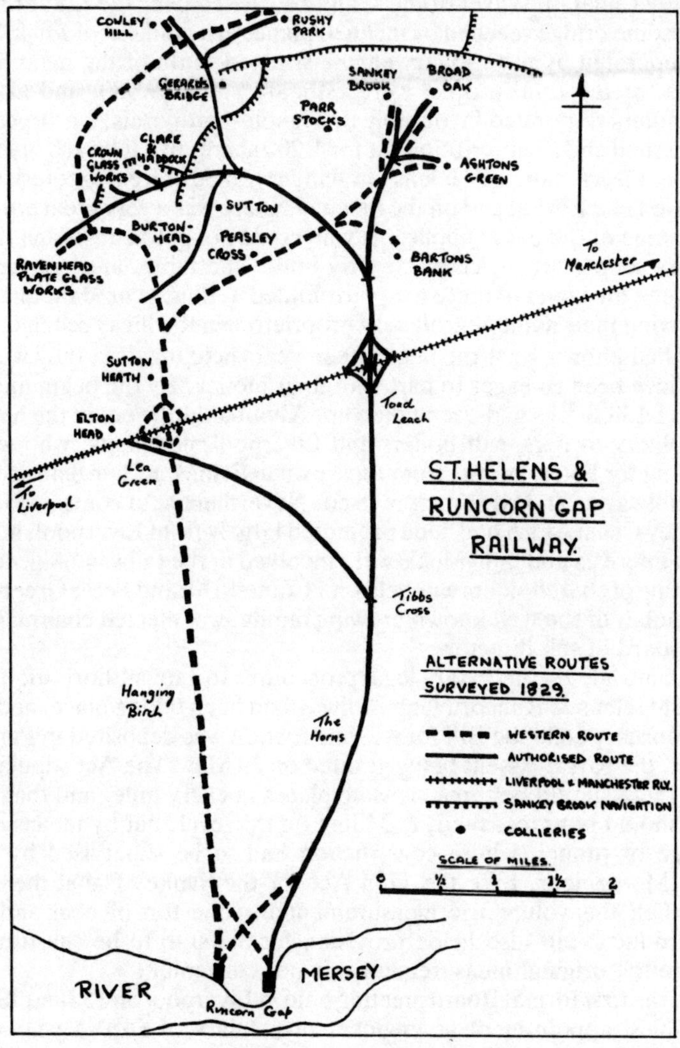

up to 300 tons, and to guarantee the necessary volume of traffic, Vignoles was asked to provide branches to most of the collieries in the area. Aided by H S Merrett and C G Forth, he surveyed two separate routes, which appear on the Parliamentary plans deposited in November 1829. In his formal report, however, he recommended the eastern route via Toad Leach and Bold Mill, which had branches serving eleven collieries and works, and no less than five connections to the L & M, near what was then known as the "foot of Sutton Incline", but which we know as St Helens Junction. The railway was to cross the Sankey Canal on swivel bridges, and be carried over the L & M by a handsome bridge reached by inclined planes at a gradient of 1 in 29/30, and operated by a stationary engine situated south of the main line. Costs for the total project were estimated at £119,980, and as the promoters responded favourably to Vignoles' proposals, a prospectus was issued and a subscription list for 1,200 shares of £100 each opened at the Fleece Inn, St Helens, in January 1830. Great interest was aroused in the area, and on the first day "there was a very great crowd, and some of the eager applicants who could not get near to sign their names soon enough, crept cleverly under the table, and, emerging between the knees of those who surrounded it, thus secured the chance of having their names enrolled as proprietors in the lucky scheme." If they had known what the next fifteen years held in store, they would not have been so eager to part with their money. By the beginning of June 1,130 shares had been taken up. About a third were in the hands of colliery owners, salt boilers and Liverpool merchants, who were looking for better profits from their own activities, rather than seeing the railway as an investment in itself. Nevertheless, in contrast to the Sankey Canal which had been promoted largely from Liverpool, many local interests and individuals were involved in the railway. A general meeting of shareholders was held on 11 June 1830, and Peter Greenall, a member of the well known brewing family, was elected chairman of the board of ten directors.

Meanwhile the necessary legal procedures to gain authorisation for the St Helens & Runcorn Gap Railway had been taking place, and on 16 February 1830 the Bill for its construction was deposited in Parliament, the Royal Assent being granted on 29 May. The Act stipulated that there should be three crossing places in every mile, and that the line should not cross the L & M line on the level, but by means of a bridge or tunnel, whose construction had to be supervised by the L & M engineer. Like the 1755 Act for the Sankey Canal the Act specified the volumetric measurement for one ton of coal and its by-products, but also made provision for 3,360 lb to be substituted where the original measurement was not convenient.

At the first formal Board meeting held in Liverpool on 15 June 1830, Vignoles' appointment as engineer at a salary of £650 a year was confirmed, but from this seemingly generous sum he was expected to pay part of the salary of his subordinate engineers, together with the expenses of surveyors and dock engineers. Although the railway was only to be single track, the directors decided at their next meeting to purchase sufficient land to cater for double track at some future date between Runcorn Gap and the crossing over the Sankey Canal in St Helens, and between Broad Oak and the junction with the L & M line. Priestley's "Historical Account of the Navigable Rivers, Canals and Railways throughout Great Britain" published in 1831, records that the total projected length of the railway, including branches and connections, was 15 miles 4 furlongs 8 chains.

Meanwhile the proprietors of the Sankey Canal had finally realised that with a direct rail link from St Helens to a dock on the River Mersey, the very survival of their waterway depended on the construction of their oft-deferred extension to Runcorn Gap. Parliamentary sanction for this was obtained on the same day that the railway was authorised. The new Act effectively reconstituted the undertaking with a nominal capital of £96,000, and confirmed the various tolls and exemptions of the 1755 and 1762 Acts, so that the maximum toll over the total length of the canal, including the new extension, remained at 1s 0d. The extension, just over 2¼ miles in length and engineered by Francis Giles, did not end in a true dock at the riverside, but at twin locks 79ft x 20ft in size, which were provided with paved surrounds to act as wharves. It was decided that the locks at Fidlers Ferry should be kept open for the convenience of traffic to and from Warrington, and to relieve congestion at Runcorn Gap at busy periods, but the old lock at Sankey Bridges gradually fell into disuse. As the locks at Runcorn Gap were adjacent to the projected railway dock, and therefore subject to the same vagaries of wind and tide, the proprietors no doubt felt that with the safeguard of the old locks up the river they could face any future competition with equanimity.

Vignoles, despite continual difficulties with landowners, had started to stake out the land for the railway. He and John Stewart, one of the directors, were authorised to place contracts for the construction of the line, which was divided into three sections for this purpose. The contract for the first section of the line north of the L & M and the northern connection thereto was awarded to J & J Thornton, but the sum involved, £15,800, was not mentioned in the minutes until some fourteen months later. The directors also requested detailed plans and estimates for the dock at Runcorn Gap, as its construction would be lengthy and complex compared to that of the railway. After seeking confirmation of Vignoles' estimates from an independent consulting engineer, Alexander Nimmo, they agreed the sum of £36,000 at a site meeting on 15 October 1830. At the same meeting they agreed that the contract for the second section of railway, which included the southern connections to the L & M, and the main line southward to what was then known as the Horns, not far from the present Farnworth & Bold station, should be let to William & Benjamin Seed at their quotation of £24,700.

Vignoles quickly pursued quotations for the supply of stone for the docks, which was awarded to Nowell & Sons of Dewsbury in November 1830, and in January of the following year the same contractor was awarded the contract for the construction of the dock for £37,000. In due course the contract for the third section of railway from the Horns to Runcorn Gap was let to J & J Thornton for £20,000.

By the middle of 1831 it had become obvious that the railway and dock would cost far more than originally estimated, and on 31 August Vignoles was asked to reappraise the whole project and assess what savings could be made. He attacked this challenge with his customary vigour, and on 10 October presented his findings to the directors. He cut out all stretches of double track south of the L & M line with the exception of the passing loops stipulated in the enabling act, and the double track on the inclined planes. He further recommended the deletion of several colliery branches, and the retention of only one connection to the L & M. These, coupled with economies in the size of the dock and its facilities, would save about £30,000, but were offset by increased costs, so after all his labour he was back to £119,000, very close to one of his original estimates.

Vignoles assured the directors that he could complete the railway and docks by the summer of 1832, without exceeding the original budgets. Work continued steadily, and the first section of line from St Helens to a junction with the L & M line was opened on 2 January 1832, using a locomotive and waggons hired from the L & M. Notwithstanding the use of the 'long' ton in the enabling act, the directors fixed the tariff for coal traffic over this stretch at 6d per imperial ton. Traffic on this section was only light, and the directors looked forward with impatience to the opening of the main line. But progress on the dock was very slow, and Mr Nowell was summoned several times to board meetings to account for delays. By the end of July 1832 there was still much to be done, but he promised that the dock would be ready by Christmas Day 1832.

On 27 July 1832, Peter Greenall had to tell the shareholders that, despite the economies initiated in the previous year, £100,883 had already been expended in the construction of the line, and as it was estimated that a further £49,101 would be needed, it would be necessary to raise the whole of the £30,000 loan authorised by the 1830 Act. Further depressing news was that although the remaining sections of the railway could be completed in about two months, the building of the dock would take much longer, and it was reasonably certain that no coal would be shipped that year.

Construction of the railway continued slowly, and even though the directors wanted the line complete by 12 November, this deadline was not met. Nevertheless, they could take some consolation that, as a result of a wager between a coal merchant and the resident engineer of the Sankey Canal, the first train carrying coal passed over the whole line from Broad Oak Colliery to the Mersey on 28 November 1832. This augured well for the official opening which, after some anxious discussion, was set for 21 February 1833. Meanwhile the tariff for the conveyance of coal over the full length of the line was set at 1s 8d per 'long' ton, despite the earlier decision to use the imperial ton for traffic to the L & M line.

All was not well, however, and the opening was an almost complete fiasco:

> "The Directors met on the line and proceeded with several waggons of coal from the Broad Oak Colliery belonging to Messrs. Bournes & Company to the Dock, where a vessel was in readiness for the cargo, but Messrs Lee Watson & Co having failed in their agreement to complete the Tipping Machine at the dock wall, the coal could not be shipped. The Stationary Engine was also incomplete though the whole were undertaken by Messr Lee Watson to be ready by this day . . . and the coals were obliged to be drawn up the Incline Plane at Sutton by Locomotive Engine and also by Men and Horses."

The directors then proceeded to deal with the contractors in no uncertain terms, and Lee Watson had the stationary engine ready by 4 March. Work on the dock was still painfully slow, and although it was filled with water in April 1833 and could admit boats of up to 300 tons burthen, it was not until 26 July that the company was able to announce that . . . "the Dock itself is complete and available for all purposes of business. The quantity shipped at the Dock from the first of this month averages upwards of 200 tons a day." Trade obviously built up quickly, for at the end of August 1833 the 'Liverpool Mercury' reported that it was commonplace to ship 400-600 tons a day. As the dock could hold more than 40 vessels, it was calculated that its capacity could be as high as 1,200-1,300 tons per day. "As a proof of the facilities accorded for despatch, a vessel has been brought into dock, seventy tons of coal discharged into her from the waggons, and in forty minutes again has been standing with all her sails set, down the channel for Liverpool."

By yet another of the coincidences which were to link canal and railway, the Sankey Brook Navigation's extension to Runcorn Gap, together with its twin locks, was opened on 24 July 1833, so both companies were ready for the struggle at the same time.

The opening of the dock was obviously a relief to the railway directors, as throughout the early part of 1833 they had been forced to make regular payments to the contractors, while very little income was being derived from the limited traffic. Vignoles worked hard at settling the final accounts, and had particular problems with Nowell & Sons because of the various changes and economies forced upon him by the company's need to minimise costs. Despite an apparently final settlement of £31,700 for their work, Nowell took legal action against the railway, whose parlous financial state had forced it through a variety of fund raising exercises, culminating on 26 March 1834 in Parliamentary sanction to raise £40,000 by means of a mortgage.

A price war which neither could afford was not long in beginning between canal and railway. The canal soon allowed 45 tons to be carried for the same rate as 40 tons had been carried previously, and on 5 April 1834 the railway retaliated by reducing its tariff by 2d a ton. At the shareholders' meeting on 28 July Peter Greenall gave details of the railway's countermeasures to the canal's surreptitious price cuts, and also stated that he had informed the Trustees of the Weaver Navigation, since that company's receipts were adversely affected as certificates of cargo made out on the Sankey were also valid on the Weaver.

He also gave details of the final estimates for the construction of the railway, which were in excess of £190,000, and thus not covered even with the mortgage. Nevertheless, he said that despite problems in construction and delays in the delivery of locomotives, which meant that horse traction was still necessary for some operations, the situation would soon improve. He was forced to admit that only three collieries were shipping through the railway dock, but stated that another would start very shortly. With boundless optimism he announced that the Ravenhead branch would be completed in six to eight weeks, although the work had been put out to tender less than a month previously. Traffic had risen to 74,460 tons in the year ending 30 June 1834, with no less than 39,763 tons carried in the second six months. The Ravenhead branch was opened in December 1834, and as it served the largest glassworks in the country, as well as other major industrial concerns, it quickly became the most important branch on the system.

In October 1834 the directors decided to investigate the use of a contractor to operate the railway. A speedy response to their enquiries came from John Jones of the Viaduct Foundry, Newton-le-Willows. He proposed to charge 1d per ton per mile for carriage from the collieries in St Helens to Runcorn Gap, and suggested that to simplify matters the distance of each colliery to the latter point should be taken as seven miles. He asked for a three year contract, with a guaranteed annual payment of £70 per week or 400 tons per working day at 7d per ton. For this he wanted full use of locomotive and stationary engines, together with the company workshops, and undertook to keep everything in good repair or replace it. The directors thought this an eminently suitable scheme, and Jones took over operations from 15

December 1834. Nevertheless operations did not markedly improve, and complaints continued about the lack of locomotive power and the increasing difficulties of operating the inclined planes, particularly as on occasions traffic reached 1,000 tons per day. A scheme to reduce the gradient of the Widnes Incline from 1 in 29 to 1 in 100 was prepared in November 1837, but soon abandoned. Matter became so desperate that colliery owners even offered to make a contribution to the cost of the new locomotives, and Jones was forced to give them a rebate when they had to use their own horses to bring waggons to Sutton. At the expiry of Jones' contract, the directors decided to take back the running of the railway into their own hands, and Thomas Lunt was appointed as Superintendent of Locomotive Power at a salary of £120 pa, plus a bonus on what he could save on the contractors' costs.

As the effect of the price cuts impacted on the once prosperous canal, overtures were made in January 1838 about the possibility of an amalgamation with the railway, but the latter's shareholders rejected the proposal. Plans were already in hand for the doubling of the northern section of the line, and authority to raise a further 1,200 £20 shares was granted on 11 June 1838. New locomotives and passenger coaches were also purchased, but the shareholders' enthusiasm was somewhat dampened when a consultant engineer reported that the reduction or elimination of the inclined planes was not a practical proposition. Traffic for the year ending 30 June 1838 had reached 131,675¾ tons of coal and 4,975¾ tons of general merchandise, but this was a drop of 8,618 over the previous year, and when all working expenses and liabilities had been settled, there was a surplus of only £392 4s 0d.

A year later, still only seven pits were regularly sending coal by rail, due in part to the economies forced on Vignoles, but also because colliery owners took advantage of the price war to ship their coal by canal at a cheaper rate, and avoid the costs and problems of transhipment at Runcorn Gap. They were aided in this by an extensive network of tramways acting as canal feeders, of which the most important were the Gerard Railway mentioned earlier, and the Stocks Railway, which ran 2½ miles from Blackleyhurst Colliery to the canal at Blackbrook.

By early 1839 traffic on the railway had declined alarmingly, and a loss of £500 was incurred. Track maintenance had suffered badly, and the directors decided once more to find contractors to work and maintain the line. Brocklehurst Nelson & Co were appointed in March 1840, but things did not improve, and by May of the following year they had gone bankrupt.

In due course a local man, Robert Daglish Junior, was appointed as contractor on a seven year contract from 1 August 1841. He refused to accept liability for any accidents during the first few months of his contract, and made the following comment a fortnight after he started:

"There are not less than 2,000 rails over which it is really dangerous to pass even with a coal waggon containing 3½ tons of coals, therefore you will readily conceive the danger incurred by the weight of the Engines varying as they do from 10 to 12 tons each."

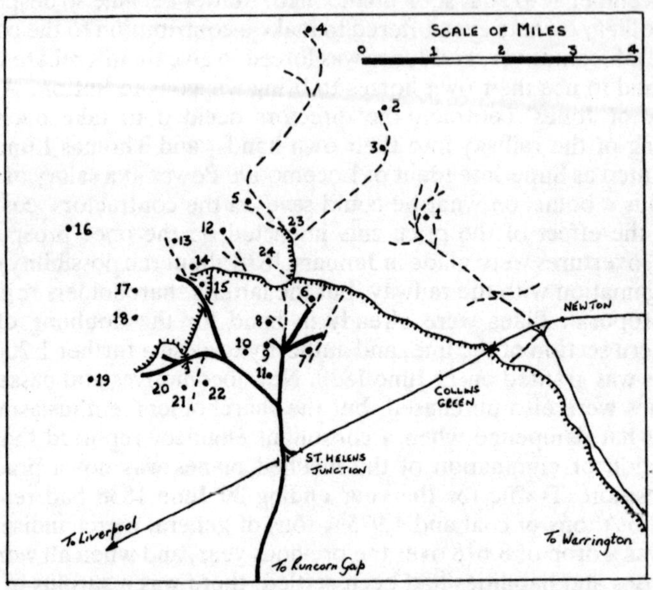


ST. HELENS SHOWING MAIN COLLIERIES AND TRAMWAYS FROM A PLAN PREPARED FOR THE 1847 PARLIAMENTARY SESSION

| | |
|---|---|
| ST. HELENS RAILWAY | LNWR |
| ST. HELENS CANAL | COLLIERY TRAMWAYS |

• COLLIERIES

| | | | |
|---|---|---|---|
| 1. | HAYDOCK | 12. | RUSHY PARK |
| 2. | HILLOCK | 13. | BIG COWLEY HILL |
| 3. | PEWFALL | 14. | COWLEY HILL |
| 4. | BLACKLEYHURST | 15. | GERARD'S BRIDGE |
| 5. | LAFFAK | 16. | WINDLE |
| 6. | BROAD OAK | 17. | GREEN LANE |
| 7. | ASHTONS GREEN | 18. | UNION |
| 8. | SANKEY BROOK | 19. | ECCLESTON ROYAL |
| 9. | PARR STOCKS | 20. | RAVENHEAD |
| 10. | SMITHFIELD | 21. | BURTONHEAD |
| 11. | BARTONS BANK | 22. | SUTTON (PEASLEY CROSS) |

23. STANLEY
24. BLACKBROOK

## CHAPTER III

# AMALGAMATION AND EXPANSION

Although the abortive amalgamation attempt of 1838 had been shelved, the possibility of a merger was still attractive to the canal and railway directors, as successive price cuts reduced the viability of their operations. In 1843 the canal company made one further attempt to resolve the difficulties of river access at Runcorn Gap by surveying an extension to Warrington, which would not only give better access to the river itself, but also to the Mersey & Irwell Navigation and the lucrative markets of Manchester. Nothing came of this scheme, or of a further project in the following year to build a railway across Warrington from the canal to the River Mersey, and events moved swiftly to bring together the Sankey Brook Navigation Canal and the St Helens & Runcorn Gap Railway. In January 1844, a formal memorandum was prepared: "At a meeting held this day between Sir Edward Cust, Thomas Case and S H Thompson on the part of the Sankey Canal Coy, and Joseph Crosfield and Gilbert Greenall on the part of the St Helens Rly Coy, it was mutually agreed that the gentlemen now present should recommend to their respective boards the sale of the Sankey Navigation to the Railway Company at and for the price of £300 for each of their 480 shares."

As the price referred to the £200 shares created by the 1830 Act, and so represented £1,200 for each of the original £155 shares, the canal shareholders accepted with alacrity. The railway directors considered that £270 per share would be a fairer figure, but they formally agreed on 31 January 1844 to purchase the waterway for £144,000. This was to be financed by the creation of 1,440 new 5 per cent preference shares, of which the canal proprietors would retain 480 on a one for one basis. The purchase was to be deemed to have taken place from 1 January 1844, and to be free of all debts, except for the canal bond debt of £29,450.

The combined enterprise was to be known as the St Helens Canal & Railway Company: the Amalgamation Bill received the Royal Assent a year later on 21 July 1845: capital of £144,000 was authorised, with power to raise up to £30,000 in loans.

The virtual monopoly created in the area by the amalgamation enabled the two rival forms of transport to share in a period of reasonable prosperity, and to remain independent for almost twenty years, despite pressures from several larger railway companies and gradual encirclement by the LNWR — a giant as yet unborn. It may appear strange that the canal should seek amalgamation with the somewhat ramshackle railway company, but the price cutting in which both concerns has indulged had reduced even the canal dividends to only 5½ per cent, while the railway had often been on the verge of bankruptcy. The docks of both concerns at Runcorn Gap had not been as successful as anticipated for, at 'neap' tides they could only be entered by fully laden vessels for two hours at each high tide, and were totally inaccessible for some 80 days a year.

Nevertheless in the ten years up to 1846 the yearly freight tonnage carried on the railway had risen from about 130,000 tons to 283,219 tons, of which coal accounted for all except 41,232 tons. Traffic on the canal had shown an even more spectacular rise from about 170,000 tons in 1836 to 440,784 tons in 1845, much of this additional tonnage coming from the new pits in the Blackbrook area where the railway had yet to penetrate.

A statement of the consolidated financial situation of the two companies for the 18 months up to 30 June 1845, as presented to the shareholders on 5 August 1845, may help to set the scene for the new enterprise:

| | £ | s | d |
|---|---|---|---|
| Income for Canal from Tonnages, Rents etc. | 21,373 | 7 | 4 |
| Expenses | 7,792 | 9 | 0 |
| Surplus | 13,580 | 18 | 4 |
| Railway Income from all sources | 17,335 | 7 | 5 |
| Expenses | 11,649 | 11 | 11 |
| Surplus | 5,685 | 15 | 6 |
| Total Surplus | 19,266 | 13 | 10 |
| Deduct Canal Bond Debt Interest @ 4% on £29,450 | 1,767 | 0 | 0 |
| Deduct Railway Bond Debt Interest @ 5% on £69,580 | 5,218 | 10 | 0 |
| Ditto on balance of purchase money due to Canal Co @ 5% | 5,150 | 4 | 11 |
| Leaving | 7,130 | 18 | 11 |
| As required by the Recent Act, the Directors propose to: | | 0 | 0 |
| Declare 5% dividend on 480 shares deemed to be fully paid up from 1.1.44 | 3,600 | | |
| and on 960 shares which are 20% paid from 1.3.44 | 1,200 | 0 | 0 |
| Leaving | 2,330 | 18 | 11 |
| Deduct total loss from opening of Railway until 31.12.43 | 1,813 | 3 | 7 |
| Final Surplus | 517 | 15 | 4 |

Peter Greenall, as the chairman of the combined undertaking, went over this somewhat gloomy picture in some detail, but pointed out that the previous year's operations had in fact produced a surplus of £1,112 12s 7d after all working expenses and loan interest had been paid. By the next meeting in February 1846 Gilbert Greenall, who had become chairman on his brother Peter's death in the previous September, was able to announce that the overall cash in hand had increased to £3,876 17s 7d, while the capital so far raised amounted to a not inconsiderable £385,602 17s 1d.

Meanwhile the town of St Helens itself, with 20,570 inhabitants, had almost doubled in size in twenty years, and it was estimated that by 1846 some 400,000 tons of coal were being consumed each year by local factories, many taking up to 30,000 tons each, a considerable short haul traffic for canal and railway. To stimulate this still further, a reduction of 1d per ton in the railway toll was made from 1 October 1845.

The glass industry in the area, although still small in comparison with that on Tyneside or in the Midlands, had continued to develop. The giant Ravenhead works still dwarfed everything else, but the opening of the St Helens Crown Glass Works in February 1827 marked the start of the firm, which we today know as Pilkington Brothers Limited. Other glass works were also established, and after 1830 the copper smelters came back to the town to bring added trade to the railway and canal. A new industry which was to grow rapidly in the area, and to cause much offence by its noxious vapours and waste products, was the alkali industry, which was originally developed to supply the soap trade with soda.

### *Expansion Plans are Laid*

In this polluted atmosphere of burgeoning industry an efficient transport system had become of paramount importance, and the directors were very conscious of the shortcomings of their railway and its operations. So in July 1845 they engaged James Meadows Rendel, a well known civil engineer, to carry out a survey of transport needs in south west Lancashire, and recommend improvements to canal and railway. His terms of reference covered improvements to the inclined planes and docks, together with extensions to Blackbrook and towards Liverpool. More fanciful aspects were covered in the instructions "to consider the practicability of the line or any portion of it becoming a link in the passenger line to the north," and the provision of junctions to any projected railways in the area.

In an interim report at the beginning of September Rendel strongly recommended lines from Parr to Wigan, and from Runcorn Gap to Garston Salt Works at an estimated cost of £240,000. He suggested that both docks at Runcorn Gap should be abandoned in favour of a dock at Garston, where coal could be loaded into boats from staithes, which would increase the speed of turn-round with less risk of breakages. Although this scheme was attractive, and the directors soon set in motion the purchase of the land for the docks at Garston, Rendel had as yet come up with nothing to improve the fundamental problems of the inclined planes. These were only able to deal with six loaded waggons of four ton gross weight at any one time, and as speed was limited to seven miles an hour, no advantage could be taken of advances in motive power since the opening of the line.

Rendel felt that the problem of the inclined planes could not be satisfactorily resolved by levelling, and in what became known as the 'Sankey Valley Scheme', he advised the abandonment of almost the whole of the existing railway in favour of an entirely new line. This would run from a point near Gerard's Bridge in St Helens to Runcorn Gap via Sankey Bridges, for the most part along the course of the Sankey Canal. When taken in conjunction with a second new line running alongside the Blackbrook branch of the canal, it would have the added advantage that all loaded coal trains would be running on a down gradient. Moreover, by building a short connection in Warrington to the projected Birkenhead, Lancashire & Cheshire Junction Railway, of which Rendel was also engineer, it would be possible to gain access to Cheshire without the need to cross the Mersey at Runcorn.

As this was the year of the "Railway Mania", the directors were carried away by rather grandiose ideas. So at the board meeting on 8 December 1845 they formally ratified plans for a branch from St Helens to Rainford, or at least a lease of the projected and recently authorised GJ branch to the same place, a line from Gerard's Bridge to Eccleston Four Lane Ends, and a connection to the GJ main line at Winwick Quay near the canal workshops. Plans had already been deposited for what was virtually a completely new dock and railway at an estimated cost of £330,000. But before the necessary Parliamentary procedures could take place, the company had to deposit £30,000 with the Bank of England as a gesture of good faith, and this was only achieved after some hard bargaining with various financiers. In February 1846 Rendel presented a report on his project to the shareholders, and pointed out that the cost of motive power, which amounted to over 60 per cent of the railway's operating cost, was nearly three times what it should be. If the existing line were extended to Blackbrook, a mere 1½ miles, it would cost another £100,000, and involve yet another inclined plane. He estimated that his Sankey Valley scheme, which was 28 miles long including branches, could be built in its entirety for about the same cost. Its only disadvantage, he admitted, was that it would be 4½ miles longer than the existing line. His proposals were enthusiastically accepted by the meeting, which endorsed the action of

# ST. HELENS & RUNCORN-GAP RAILWAY CO.

From this Date, the hours of Departure from this Station, will be as follows until further Notice.

*Railway Office, St. Helens, October 14th, 1842.*

## TIMES OF DEPARTURE FROM SAINT HELENS STATION.

### To Manchester.

Quarter-past 7, 10 o'clock, quarter-past 2, and a quarter before 6.

*Fares Inside, 4s.—Outside, 3s.*

### To Liverpool.

Quarter-past 8, quarter before 11, quarter-past 2, half-past 3, and a quarter before 6.

*Fares Inside, 2s. 6d.—Outside, 2s.*

### To Bolton.

* Quarter-past 7, 10 * quarter-past 2, and a quarter before 6.

*Fares Inside, 4s. 0d.—Outside, 3s. 0d.*

### To Wigan.

Quarter-past 7, * 10 o'clock, * quarter-past 2, and a * quarter before 6

*Fares Inside, 4s —Outside, 3s.*

### To Preston.

* Quarter-past 7, * 10 o'clock, * quarter-past 2, and a * quarter before 6

*Fares Inside, 7s.—Outside, 5s. 6d.*

### To Warrington.

Quarter-past 7, half-past 3, and a quarter before 6.

*Fares Inside, 3s—Outside, 2s.*

### To Birmingham, London, &c.

Persons willing to wait a short time at Warrington, may go by the Trains at a quarter-past 7, half-past 3, and a quarter before 6.

Also by waiting at Parkside or Kenyon Junction about half and hour Persons may go by the Wigan and Bolton Trains marked *.

### On Sundays.

To all the above named places, at a quarter-past 7, A. M. and a quarter before 6, P. M.

### To Southport, via. Ormskirk.

Edward Fidler's Patent Safety Coaches leave St. Helens Station for Southport every Day, (Sundays excepted) on the arrival of the two o'clock Train from Manchester.

*Passengers and Parcels Booked for Southport, at the Liverpool and Manchester Railway Co's Offices, Market Street, and Liverpool Road, Manchester.*

*Fares to Southport, Inside, 10s.—Outside, 7s.*

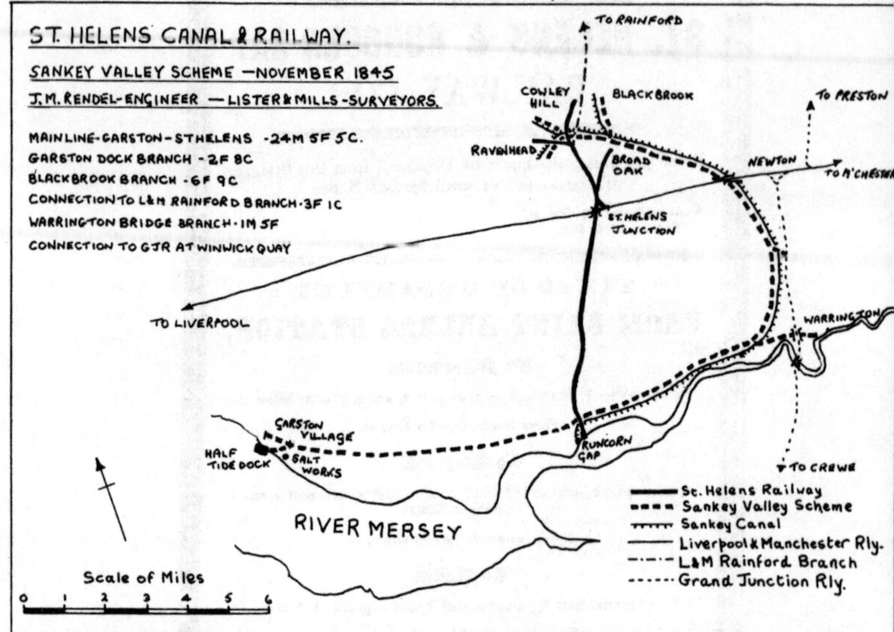


the directors in laying all the schemes so speedily before Parliament.

The Parliamentary Committee was not so easy to convince, annd bitter opposition to the project was voiced by the Grand Junction particularly as far as the Eccleston branch was concerned, because of its strategic importance if the GJ plans to build a line from Huyton to St Helens came to fruition. On 15 May 1846 the St Helens directors decided to withdraw this part of their scheme to mollify the GJ, but in spite of a spirited fight for the remainder, only the seven mile line from Runcorn Gap to Garston was sanctioned. The Royal Assent was given on 16 July 1846, authorising capital of £240,000 and loans of up to £80,000, with the stipulation that the works had to be completed within five years and the docks at Runcorn Gap kept open.

The rejection of the Sankey Valley scheme meant that improvements to the existing railway were once more a priority, and Rendel was instructed to devote all his energies to the problems of this line which, from evidence given before the Gauge Commissioners in 1845, was ten miles in length, with four miles of the 60lb rails laid on stone blocks and the remainder on transverse sleepers. It was also recorded that there were no tunnels or viaducts on the existing lines, but merely ten overbridges and two underbridges.

Rendel was not left undisturbed to formulate his improvement plans, as the minds of the directors were still full of new schemes for extensions to the system. So on 5 September 1846, in addition to preparing detailed estimates for the Garston line, he was instructed to draw up plans for a line from Runcorn Gap to Warrington, together with an extension from Garston into Liverpool.

Out of all the confusion Rendel managed to prepare an estimate of £160,000 to cover new construction, as well as a scheme to reduce the inclined planes to 1 in 100, so that locomotive engines could be used for the whole distance. In retrospect it is easy to be critical of the directors, but in the last two years they had achieved amalgamation with their arch rival, the Sankey Canal, and had seen all their neighbours swallowed up first by the GJ and then by the LNWR, while a proliferation of railway schemes in all directions was constantly before their eyes. One thing was certain, however, if they could capitalise on the amalgamation, improve their railway operations and tap new markets by judicious expansion, they at last had the opportunity to create a viable enterprise.

Nevertheless the company had pressing financial problems, not merely in its day-to-day operations, but also to facilitate the purchase of as much land as possible for the proposed Warrington extension and thus reduce any opposition before the Parliamentary hearing. The scheme envisaged a line just under six miles in length, starting from an end-on junction with the Garston line at Runcorn Gap, some five furlongs to the east of the St Helens line, and terminating at a station in Bridge Street, Warrington. There was also to be a short connection to the BLCJ, and a further short branch to the LNWR line north of Bank Quay station, although this latter proposal was later withdrawn.

The other important new line was 1 mile 33¼ chains in length, and would run from the existing Broad Oak branch to a terminus to the west of the head of the Blackbrook branch of the Sankey Canal. Almost one million tons of coal were now being raised annually in the St Helens area, but whereas the salt trade could make do with small coal, higher quality fuel was required particularly for steam ships, so new collieries were being sunk to tap the rich Rushy Park seam north east of St Helens, and the Blackbrook line was intended to give the railway access to these.

Despite the opposition of the LNWR, which had submitted its own schemes for lines to Rainford, Ormskirk, St Helens, Warrington and Blackbrook, modifying some of those authorised in the previous two years, the St Helens Railway was successful in getting all its project through the Commons, including the leasing of the proposed LNWR Rainford branch. In all, just over seven miles of new railway were authorised, together with three miles of deviations to modify the inclined planes. The Royal Assent was given on 22 July 1847, when capital of £159,400 was sanctioned, together with loans of £53,100.

Official records show that at this time the St Helens Railway employed 112 staff and owned nine locomotives, but although over 400 waggons were to be found on its metals, a mere twenty belonged to the company, with the remainder owned by colliery owners and other industrialists. Sixteen miles of canal were in operation, and by the end of 1850 almost twelve miles of railway, of which seven were double track, would be in use. But the most pressing problem was to improve operations on the original line, whose major obstacles were described in the 1847 Act as "two inclined planes, one of which worked by stationary engine and the other by self-acting machinery, which entail great expense upon the Company and delay in the traffic of the said Railway". Robert Daglish Jnr, who at that time was still the contractor responsible for the operation of the railway, put forward tenders in line with Rendel's plans for the deviations to eliminate the Widnes and Sutton inclines. Both were about 1½ miles long and enabled the gradients to be reduced to between 1 in 94 and 1 in 105. Daglish's tenders were accepted in July 1847, and he was also authorised to buy the pulleys and stationary engine from the Sutton Incline, although the old rails, chains and ropes were to remain the property of the company. The engine house at Sutton was soon to fall into disuse, but remained standing until the 1880s, and was only demolished when the original bridge across the L & M line was replaced by the present structure. Daglish was given an advance of £1,000 to start work on the Sutton Incline, but it was decided to leave the Widnes incline for the time being. Indeed, on 1 November 1847 Daglish was told to proceed as slowly as possible with the work in hand, as the total cost of the alterations was £9,000, and the company already faced an anticipated excess of expenditure over income in the following half year.

Notwithstanding the financial problems, the directors were still keen on the Liverpool extension, and asked Rendel to survey a suitable route. He and Nathaniel Beardmore, a former pupil, produced plans for a line just under 5½ miles in length to run from a junction on the projected Garston line, and continue on a more or less level course through Otterspool, before passing under Dingle Lane in a 1,069 yard tunnel. There was to be a short branch to Queens Dock, while the main line, after crossing the LNWR Park Lane (Wapping) goods line on a 56 arch viaduct, faced a sharp 1 in 40 climb to the projected terminus in Canning Place. But, although nothing came of this scheme, the idea of a line from Garston to Liverpool was to be an obsession with the St Helens Railway (and other companies) throughout the fifties and early sixties. For the moment, however, the company found itself unable to complete the lines for which it already had authority, and the directors were forced to apply to the Railway Commissioners for an extension of the powers of the 1846 Act, so that the Garston line could be built. In fact the only line on which there was any real activity in the next two years was built without specific Parliamentary sanction.

*New Lines are Completed*

The meagre facilities of the original station in St Helens, which was near Peasley Cross, were becoming increasingly congested by the heavy cross traffic to and from the Ravenhead branch. This, coupled with complaints from local residents about the dangers and delays at the adjacent level crossing, made the directors look at providing a new station and offices nearer the town centre. An ideal site was found opposite the Raven Inn in Raven Street, as this required only the extension of an existing line across the canal to reach ample space for terminal facilities for both passengers and freight. Work started in February 1849 and progressed steadily, so that on 15 October, the Secretary was instructed to write to the Railway Commissioners and inform them that the line, which was 21¾ chains long, would be ready for opening in ten days' time. The Board of Trade inspector, Captain Laffan RE, was not at all pleased with what he found, and he also passed some scathing comments on the existing line, for on his journey from St Helens Junction he had noted "that the permanent way was in very bad order, and that some of the junctions with the coal lines were effected in a very rough way by means of 'shifting rails'. I am of the opinion that a line for passenger traffic should not be allowed to remain in such a state". Two further inspections were necessary, and detailed signalling instructions were provided by the Board of Trade, before the line was passed as fit for traffic. The first public train ran to the new station on 19 December 1849. Contemporary maps show the station as having thirteen lines, sidings and bays, and the directors were well satisfied with it. But a local historian, writing some forty years later, described it as a "small, rudely constructed erection". A building at the junction of Salisbury Street and Church Street, in which passenger receipts dating from this period were found at its demolition in 1959, is thought to have been the station booking office.

Meanwhile, by February 1849 the levelling of the inclined plane across the Liverpool-Manchester line at Sutton had been completed. Work started on the Widnes incline and the doubling of the rest of the main line in the following April. The impending construction of the Blackbrook branch, which was estimated to cost £13,000, caused controversy both on the grounds of expense and on the anticipated level of traffic. Some mystery also surrounded the letting of the basic construction contract to Daglish & McCormick for £8,000 in April 1849. But this was simply a manoeuvre to get Daglish to surrender his interest in the reconstruction of the Widnes incline, which the directors wished to be carried out by John Smith, who had taken over the operation of the existing line from 1 February 1849 on the expiry of

Daglish's contract. Problems were also encountered in providing satisfactory connections to the Laffak and Blackleyhurst Collieries, which operated their own tramway feeders to the canal. These mines were raising well over 50,000 tons per year each, and their proprietors had promised to send at least that amount by rail to the projected docks at Garston. Although Daglish and his partner had seemingly made a good start on the Blackbrook branch in the spring of 1849, it was not completed as a single line until towards the end of 1850. It was doubled in the spring of 1862, and later formed part of the Carr Mill avoiding line.

Another project involving somewhat protracted negotiations was a branch running from the Blackbrook line to the Haydock collieries, which had operated a private railway down to the L & M and W & N lines at Newton for the past twenty years. The St Helens Railway required 20,000 tons a year to be shipped via Runcorn Gap, and then via Garston Dock when the new facilities were ready. Agreement was reached in February 1851, and the branch completed later that year. Several other short branches to collieries and industrial undertakings were built about the same time, although financial constraints were still the order of the day. Nevertheless, for the past three years even the ordinary shareholders had received a dividend, an unknown occurrence in the railway's early years. Much of this increased prosperity was due to the canal, whose purchase was formally completed in March 1850. Despite the emphasis on railway construction and neglect even of essential maintenance, the waterway still carried the bulk of the company's freight traffic, a situation which was to persist until after the opening of the Garston branch.

This latter project, despite the first flush of enthusiasm, had certainly stagnated, and it was not until early in 1850, after considerable pressure had been exerted by local pit owners, that a start was made in earnest. Five colliery owners guaranteed a minimum of 148,500 tons per annum for shipment via Garston, and even offered to make some contribution to the construction of the line and dock, provided that the company would grant some concessions if more than 300,000 tons were shipped in any one year.

Much of the necessary land over which the land would run had already been obtained very cheaply, but the purchase of the Garston estates on which the dock and other terminal facilities were to be built, was still not finalised. In due course a price of £37,500 was agreed, and the directors suddenly wanted action. Smith and Rendel were instructed to complete detailed plans for the docks, and work began with a vengeance. On 18 November 1850 Smith was able to report that some 800 yards of track had already been laid, and a month later the directors were able to travel over ¾ mile of the Garston line. They then turned their attention to providing facilities for coal merchants along the route, particularly at Ditton, although they decided that the unloading and weighing should be carried out by railway employees at a charge of 3d per ton.

In February 1851, Gilbert Greenall was able to inform the shareholders that work had commenced on the dock, and 1¾ miles of track had already been laid. In a sudden burst of optimism he stated that, in view of the easy nature of the terrain, he saw no reason why the line should not be completed by the end of the year. This naturally threw the engineers into a turmoil, and they demanded that the men working on the dock should be increased to 500, to which the board reluctantly agreed. Stations were projected at Ditton Mill and Butchers Lane, but as the prime purpose of the line was the transport of freight, particularly coal, and the creation of a dock system to compete with the growing port of Liverpool, the directors' main concern was to expedite the construction of the dock.

Nevertheless revenue was important, so the directors decided to open the line as far as Ditton Mill. One mile 37 chains of single line was inspected on 21 May 1851 by Captain Wynne RE, who noted that it was joined to the St Helens line at Runcorn Gap by a sharp curve of ten chains radius. This was an unauthorised addition, as the Parliamentary plan had merely shown the original line being crossed on the level almost at right angles. Still, as the junction lay within the approved limits of deviation, he was prepared to overlook this. He was most scathing on the construction of the junction, and the general congestion and signalling arrangements at Runcorn Gap. He therefore deferred the opening for a month, so that these deficiencies could be rectified. Construction of the line continued apace, and in addition to the men at the dock, 289 were employed on the railway at the end of 1851, so that it could be finished by the middle of the following year. The formal opening of the full length of the Garston line took place on 1 July 1852, when a station on the new line at Waterloo Road crossing in Runcorn Gap was also taken into use. This replaced the original station, which had been situated on the St Helens line near the entrance to the docks.

Attention now focussed on the construction of the dock, where extensive coal yards had to be laid out, while warehouses and the high speed coal drops engineered by Daglish all had to be erected. The formal opening was fixed for 21 June 1853, and this was a momentous occasion with guests arriving by train, steamer and omnibus, as well as by their private means. A magnificent meal was provided for 800 people in one of the new warehouses, and the lengthy speeches did full justice to the company's achievements, while expressing the hope that the railway would soon reach the very heart of Liverpool.

The "Liverpool Mercury" for 24 June 1853, in addition to describing the festivities, went into great detail on the construction of the dock, and its proposed operation. All the stone used in its construction, except for twenty limestone blocks, had been excavated from the river bed, a lengthy and often hazardous undertaking because of the amount of mud in the approaches. The dock enclosed a total water area of just over six acres, to which entrance was gained through two colossal gates 50 ft in width. There was also a smaller entrance, basically a lock 100 ft long by 30 ft wide, which allowed access to small vessels at low water. The dock walls were 34 ft high, and the 100 ft wide wharf more than 830 yards in length. Warehouses were provided on the south quay and equipped with cranes and hydraulic waggon tipplers, by which it was estimated that 250 tons of coal could be loaded in just over two hours. Provision was made for 1,000 waggons to be accommodated within the yards, while facilities for domestic coal merchants were provided adjacent to the passenger station.

The port quickly gained a reputation for rapid and efficient turn-round, and the volume of business increased at a phenomenal rate, so that continual improvements were necessary to the facilities in the Garston area. In 1853, mainly as a result of the opening of the new line and dock, the railway tonnage rose to 613,805 against 510,668 tons carried on the Sankey — the first year in which the canal had carried less than the railway. Yet tonnages on the canal continued to increase, and it still had an important part to play in the industrial life of the area.

## CHAPTER IV

# EXTENSION TO WARRINGTON

The St Helens Railway Act of 1847 gave the local company access to the important industrial centre of Warrington, which at that time was well known for its metal working industries such as wire drawing, and the manufacture of files, pins and nails. As a glassmaking centre it was already in decline in the face of competition from St Helens, but the soap and chemical works of Joseph Crosfield — which still dominate the river bank — were already increasing in size and scope.

Warrington had long been a focal point for road transport, as it possessed the most westerly bridges over the Mersey, while on the LNW main line, which passed through the town, it was already possible to travel between London and Carlisle, as well as to Liverpool and Manchester. The first railway to reach Warrington had been the Warrington & Newton, opened throughout on 25 July 1831, although partial operations had commenced almost two months previously. It was absorbed by the Grand Junction Railway under the terms of an Act of 12 June 1835, although that major trunk line was not opened until 4 July 1837 between Birmingham and Warrington, where it made an end-on junction with the Bank Quay branch of the W & N.

Even while the St Helens Railway was contemplating its Warrington extension, several of its directors had been in discussion with members of the GJ board, and the outcome was a proposal for a Warrington & Stockport Railway, which was provisionally registered on 7 July 1845. It was to provide direct communication to Warrington from the Manchester & Birmingham Railway at Stockport, together with a junction with the still unborn Manchester South Junction & Altrincham Railway at Altrincham. Nothing came of this scheme, but the fortunes of the latter company of the same name were closely bound up with St Helens Railway and with the MSJA, which had been promoted by the M & B and Manchester, Sheffield & Lincolnshire Railways. Although the main object in constructing the MSJA was to provide a connection from the M & B to the L & M line, the so-called branch to Altrincham is of major interest in our study, as it was to form part of an alternative route between Liverpool and Manchester. The line from Oxford Road in Manchester to Altrincham was opened on 20 July 1849, and the other short sections followed within the next two months. Motive power was provided by the MS & L, with whom the St Helens Railway was to become involved on several occasions as a defence against the incursions of the LNWR.

Early in 1850 a slightly truncated version of the W & S scheme was being enthusiastically pursued by Gilbert Greenall and his colleagues, as well as local businessmen. Known as the Warrington & Altrincham Junction Railway, it was to start from an end-on junction with the St Helens Railway at Arpley on the north bank of the Mersey, and its main line, 11 miles 12 chains in length, having crossed the river by a single span bridge, was then to run via Latchford and Lymm to join the MSJA just south of that company's Timperley station. There was also to be a branch 2 miles 11 chains in length from Latchford to Lower Walton near Daresbury, to join the BLCJ line after that had crossed the LNW main line, and thus give an independent route into Warrington from Cheshire and Wales.

Three directors of the St Helens Railway, Gilbert Greenall, Charles Holland and William Charles Fosbery, were on the board of the W & A, while both the company secretary and its legal advisers performed similar functions for the St Helens Company. As Holland and Fosbery were also involved with the MS & L, the policy of the new company could easily be manipulated to further the interests of the other two companies in their struggle with the LNWR.

The Warrington & Altrincham Junction Railway was authorised on 3 July 1851 with capital of £180,000 and power to raise a further £60,000 in loans. Certain provisions worried the St Helens board, particularly the siting of the joint station in Warrington, which the Act stated should be within 150 yards of the Wilderspool Causeway, but which could be on either the north or south bank of the Mersey. By November, however, it had been decided to build it on the Lancashire side of the river, and land was obtained from John Wilson Patten, from

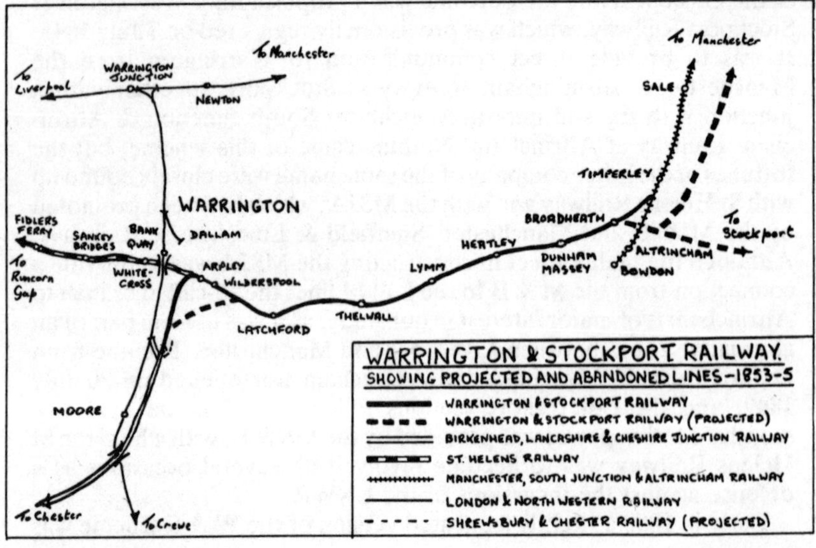

whom the St Helens Railway was also purchasing land for its Warrington branch.

Even before work was properly started, the W & A directors decided to emulate the 1845 scheme, and laid plans before Parliament to extend from Timperley to a terminus in Stockport. These were authorised on 4 August 1853, and the Act also empowered the company to change its name to the Warrington & Stockport Railway. Its dreams of a Stockport extension was never fulfilled, although some £20,000 was expended on the abortive project, and it was left to the Stockport, Timperley & Altrincham Railway, one of the constituents of the Cheshire Lines Committee, to realise this ambition in 1865-6. Meanwhile on 20 August 1853, the W & S had obtained authority to replace the proposed Latchford-Walton connection to the BLCJ by a much shorter one to the west of Arpley station, which would have the merit of putting the station on the direct line from Cheshire to Manchester. The W & S also had ambitions of extending to Manchester, and some discussions took place with the St Helens Railway, but the various schemes came to nothing.

Although the St Helens Railway's Warrington branch had been authorised in 1847, the financial problems of the post-amalgamation years, followed by the concentration on the Garston branch, caused the company to ignore what was at that stage a distinctly less promising venture. But with the opening of the BLCJ line from Chester to Walton Junction on 31 October 1850, and the authorising of the W & A in the following year, the St Helens Railway board renewed its interest in the project.

The course of its line between Runcorn Gap and Sankey Bridges was to run alongside the canal and, although the waterway had to be diverted near Fidlers Ferry, some three miles from Runcorn Gap, the survey of the levels presented little difficulty. Some work was done at the western end of the line in 1851, but as from Sankey Bridges the canal curved sharply northwards to St Helens, it course could not be used as a guide, so the final surveys of the route required more detailed attention. The LNWR was requested to raise the level of the main line bridge at Bank Quay, so that the new line could pass under it to reach the projected joint station at Arpley, about a mile to the east. As mentioned above, land for the line was to be purchased from John Wilson Patten, whose family were extremely powerful in the town, and whose residence, Bank Hall (now Warrington Town Hall), was the subject of one of the several protective clauses in the 1847 Act: "The said Company shall not erect any Station, Watchbox or other Building within sight of the Window of Bank Hall, or leave any Waggons or Carriages on the said line within sight of the said Mansion for a longer time than is absolutely requisite for the proper Management of the Traffic of the line: and a Penalty of Five Pounds will be paid to the said

John Wilson Patten, his Heirs of Assigns, for every Hour during which the said Waggons or Carriages shall be so left on the said Line."

Now that things seemed to be on the move at long last, in March 1852 the inhabitants of Penketh and Great Sankey requested the company to provide a passenger and freight station at Fidlers Ferry, adjacent to the ferry and inn which had long provided refreshments for travellers on canal and river. The winding bay for boats to turn into the lock between canal and river at this point was to be filled in to accommodate the railway, and the directors agreed to install the necessary facilities if a public carriage road was built from the Warrington-Runcorn Gap road to provide proper access.

*The St Helens Railway Reaches Warrington*

Work continued steadily on the branch, and by November 1852 it was confidently forecast that the line could be completed as far as Bank Quay by 1 January of the following year. A temporary junction had been laid in to the LNW main line at Bank Quay mainly to carry ballast, but although several schemes for effecting a permanent junction were put forward in the remaining years of the St Helens Railway's independent existence, none came to fruition. Despite a few minor delays, the opening to a temporary Warrington terminus at Whitecross took place on 1 February 1853, but over a year to elapse before it was extended to Arpley. There was no cause for alarm on that score, as the W & S was nowhere near completing its line into Warrington.

At a meeting on 25 July, the W & S directors decided to purchase their own coaching stock, but agreed that the St Helens Railway should work all their trains at a charge of 10d per mile under normal operating conditions, although a surcharge of 2d per mile would be paid for any such work before the two lines had made physical connection. The reason for the latter provision was that the bridges at either end of the W & S line, and particularly that over the Mersey at Warrington, were by no means complete. Nevertheless the W & S directors were determined that their line should open on 1 November 1853 even in isolation, with a service of four trains daily in each direction. The Board of Trade inspection took place on 25 October, with a private ceremony for directors and their friends three days later. A temporary station in Warrington was erected to the east of the level crossing at Wilderspool Causeway, and single line operation on the 'one engine in steam' principle continued until the bridges and connections were completed.

Meanwhile the St Helens Railway extension to Arpley was also nearing completion, but it was decided to delay its opening until the W & S line was complete. So on 24 April 1854 Captain Wynne had four stretches of line to inspect — the double track extensions of both companies into Warrington, the connection to the MSJA at Timperley, which was also double track, and the second track of the W & S main line. He pronounced himself satisfied with all these, and public services commenced on Monday, 1 May 1854, when the joint station at Arpley was brought into use, and the temporary stations at Wilderspool and Whitecross closed. Captain Wynne gave the length of the Whitecross-Arpley extension as 45.75 chains, and it would appear that the location of Whitecross, which was named after a nearby mediaeval preaching cross, was just east of Litton Mill crossing. It has been said that a single platfrom and waiting room survived there until the early years of this century, but there seems no documentary evidence to support this.

The W & S was to have a generally unhappy existence, heightened by the difficulties with its running powers over the MSJA and the connection to the BLCJ at Walton Junction. Despite the clause in the 1853 Act requiring the MSJA to convey passengers without change of carriage into Oxford Road, Manchester, for a period of five years, the W & S was soon in difficulty over tolls for this traffic. While the matter was at arbitration, passengers had to change at Timperley and walk 200 yards to change trains. Although the arbitrator gave the go-ahead for through trains from 1 December 1854, the W & S had to pay the following charges for each passenger: 1s 3d first class, 10½d second class, 8¾d third class — while the normal fares for the same distance were 9d, 6¾d and 5d respectively.

The connection to the BLCJ also caused problems for the W & S. These were not related to its construction, for even the 400ft single span girder bridge across the Mersey had been completed without delay and satisfactorily tested in March 1855. The Inspecting Officer was happy with the branch itself, but less so with the signalling arrangements at Walton Junction, which were necessarily complex as the lines of three companies came together at that point. These were passed off at the beginning of November, but the BLCJ still delayed the opening, because it felt the arrangements were confusing. Its obstructive attitude also combined with that of the LNWR and MSJA in preventing the operation of W & S freight services into Manchester until 25 September 1856, even though the 1853 Act had authorised the W & S to run freight trains over the line between 10 pm and 6 am.

As the W & S was operated as a virtual extension of the St Helens Railway, with three directors on the boards of both companies, its problems were bound to affect the older company. Comparative figures in 1856 show that with average receipts of £90-£120 per week its passenger traffic was about half that of the St Helens Railway, but the real difference could be seen in the freight traffic receipts for the half year ending 30 June 1856 — £156 11s 9d on the W & S, and £21,331 on the St Helens Railway.

The vexed question of the MS & L working all trains between Warrington and Garston was broached several times and rejected by the St Helens board, but agreement was reached for the MS & L to work the W & S as an extension of the MSJA for 50 per cent of the gross receipts, and this arrangement came into force from 1 October 1856. The LNWR, as a partner with the MS & L in the MSJA, was not happy about these moves which increased the threat to its monopoly of through traffic between Manchester and Merseyside, while the W & S for the last three years of its nominally independent existence was a mere pawn in the power struggle which ultimately cost the St Helens Railway its independence.

ST. HELENS RAILWAY TIME TABLE, 1859.

[FEBRUARY 1st.]

**FROM ST. HELENS**

| For Liverpool. | For Manchester. | For Bolton. | For Wigan & Preston. | For Warrington. | For Runcorn-Gap Garston and Warrington. | For Rainford. | For Ormskirk and Southport. |
|---|---|---|---|---|---|---|---|
| H. M. | H. M. | H. M. | H. M. | H. M. | H. M. | H. M. | H. M. |
| 7 0 | | | | | | | |
| 7 45 | 7 0 | 7 0 | | | | | |
| 9 30 | | | 7 45 | 7 45 | 7 25 | 8 20 | 8 20 |
| 10 30 | 9 15 | 9 15 | | | | | |
| 11 15 | | | | | 9 8 | 10 10 | 10 10 |
| 1 25 | 10 30 | 10 30 | | 11 15 | | | |
| 4 0 | | | 12 35 | 12 35 | 11 50 | | |
| 4 45 | 12 35 | 12 35 | 2 30 | | 2 8 | 1 20 | 1 20 |
| 5 45 | 2 30 | | 3 30 | | | | |
| 6 50 | 3 30 | 3 30 | | 3 30 | | 4 35 | 4 35 |
| 7 30 | 4 45 | 4 45 | 5 45 | 5 45 | 5 25 | | |
| 8 40 | 6 50 | 7 30 | 7 30 | | 7 20 | 6 20 | 6 20 |
| | 7 30 | | | 7 30 | | | |
| **SUNDAY TRAINS AS FOLLOWS:—** | | | | | | | |
| H. M. | H. M. | H. M. | H. M. | H. M. | H. M. | H. M. | H. M. |
| | 8 15 | 8 55 | | | 8 35 | 8 30 | 8 30 |
| 8 55 | 8 55 | | 8 55 | | | | |
| 9 45 | | | | 9 45 | 2 30 | 3 0 | |
| 7 30 | 7 0 | 7 0 | 7 0 | 7 0 | 7 5 | | 3 0 |
| 9 10 | 8 30 | | | 8 30 | | 7 45 | |

**TO ST. HELENS.**

| From Liverpool. | From Manchester. | From Bolton. | From Preston. | From Wigan. | From Warrington. | From Runcorn-Gap. | From Garston. | From Warrington. (by Runcorn-Gap) | From Southport. | From Ormskirk. | From Rainford. |
|---|---|---|---|---|---|---|---|---|---|---|---|
| H. M. | H. M. | H. M. | H. M. | H. M. | H. M. | H. M. | H. M. | H. M. | H. M. | H. M. | H. M. |
| 6 30 | 6 45 | 6 55 | 6 30 | 7 13 | 7 35 | | 7 40 | 7 35 | 7 45 | 8 25 | |
| 7 15 | | | 8 45 | | | 7 55 | | | | | 8 4[illegible] |
| 9 0 | 9 0 | 9 0 | 10 0 | 9 20 | 9 20 | | 9 15 | 9 20 | 9 0 | 10 5 | |
| 10 0 | 10 30 | 10 30 | | | | 9 40 | | | | | 10 2[illegible] |
| 11 15 | | | | 10 36 | | | | | 12 45 | | |
| 12 15 | 12 40 | 12 35 | 12 20 | | 2 5 | 12 20 | 11 55 | 12 0 | | 1 20 | 1 4[illegible] |
| 2 20 | | | | 12 55 | 4 3 | 2 35 | 2 10 | 2 10 | | | |
| 3 0 | 3 15 | 3 20 | | | | | | | 4 0 | | |
| 4 30 | 5 20 | | | | | | | | | 4 45 | 5 5 |
| 5 30 | | | 6 20 | | 5 0 | 5 50 | 5 30 | 5 35 | | 6 25 | 6 4[illegible] |
| 6 40 | 7 0 | 7 0 | | 6 58 | 9 0 | | 7 40 | 7 25 | | | |
| 7 15 | 8 0 | | | | | 8 1 | | | | | |
| **SUNDAY TRAINS AS FOLLOWS.—** | | | | | | | | | | | |
| H. M. | H. M. | H. M. | H. M. | H. M. | H. M. | H. M. | H. M. | H. M. | H. M. | H. M. | H. M. |
| 7 45 | 8 0 | 8 5 | 8 30 | 9 17 | 8 10 | | 8 40 | | 7 45 | 8 30 | 9 3[illegible] |
| 8 30 | 8 45 | | | | | 9 0 | 2 35 | 8 40 | | | |
| 9 30 | 6 25 | 6 30 | 6 15 | 6 58 | 5 55 | 3 0 | | 2 40 | | 3 0 | 3 2[illegible] |
| 6 25 | | | | | | | | | 7 0 | 7 40 | 3 1[illegible] |
| 8 0 | 8 30 | | | | | 7 50 | 7 15 | 7 30 | | | |

# CHAPTER V
# TURBULENT YEARS

At the half-yearly meeting of the St Helens Railway shareholders on 1 February 1851, Gilbert Greenall announced a most satisfactory upturn in business during 1850. Traffic had shown a substantial increase with 203,131 passengers booked on the line, compared with 135,420 in 1849. Freight tonnage had reached 847,587 tons on canal and railway combined, 66,356 tons up on the previous year. But, although a dividend of 25s 0d was recommended on each ordinary share, the overall financial situation was far from good, for with outstanding liabilities at £140,123, more money would have to be borrowed even to cover the annual interest payments of £3,138.

In due course it was decided to raise some of the necessary cash by selling off those parts of the Garston estate not required for railways or docks, and by the creation of another 4,800 4½ per cent preference shares, which would provide £120,000 to see the company through its immediate problems. Rather surprisingly the 1853 Act, which authorised the construction of the Rainford and Eccleston branches and improvements to the station at Sutton, did not call for any further capital, and its only financial provision was to consolidate the existing shares of the company.

Early in 1853 the St Helens Improvement Commissioners announced their intention to improve Peasley Cross Lane, and focussed attention on the proliferation of lines in that area which, despite the construction of the new station in 1849, still caused considerable disruption to road traffic and danger to unwary pedestrians. This was ultimately solved by passing all the lines over a single bridge across Peasley Cross Lane. A new curve between the St Helens and Garston lines at Runcorn Gap to improve the interchange of traffic at that point was also planned, but was not completed and passed by the the Board of Trade until November 1856. Additional station facilities described as 'a small cottage and platform', were sanctioned at both Bold and Clock Face on 17 October 1853, but the former had only a short life as it appeared for the last time in "Bradshaw" in January 1858.

Perhaps the most significant domestic event in the early fifties occurred on 1 September 1854 with the appointment of a young Scot, James Cross, to fill the ponderously-named post of Resident Engineer and Outdoor Superintendent of Traffic, although Rendel remained nominally Engineer-in-Chief until his death in 1856. Cross's achievements are perhaps greatest in the locomotive field and will be covered later, but he was also a competent civil engineer. His first task with the comany was to lay a second line of rails from the old station up to Gerard's Bridge, as traffic was expected to increase with the opening of several new factories in the area, but other priorities intervened, and this line was also not passed for traffic until November 1856.

Finance remained a major problem for the company, and in July 1856 it was decided to apply for powers to raise £100,000 in extra capital, together with £30,000 in loans. By February 1857 revenue had more than doubled since 1849, but out of the gross receipts of £40,398 for the second half of 1856, only £299 7s 4d was left to be carried over to the following year after payment of interest charges and dividends. 584,241 passengers were carried on the railway, an increase of almost 50,000 over 1855. Coal and merchandise traffic on the railway was 706,150 tons and on the canal 629,563, a grand total of 1,335,703 tons, and an increase of 132,429 tons over the previous year.

Although traffic through Garston was not growing as quickly as had been hoped, Gilbert Greenall estimated that some newly acquired business in the China trade would enable the total income of the company to reach £100,000 per annum in 1858.

The St Helens Railway had originally refused to open a station at Cuerdley on the Warrington line, but its inhabitants were extremely persistent, and in November 1855 it was announced that their request had been granted. Unfortunately, Cuerdley, admirably situated near the bone works midway between Runcorn Gap and Fidlers Ferry, was very definitely unprofitable. On 5 January 1858, despite pleas from the residents, the directors ordered it to be closed, and to avoid any repetition of the fiasco set a minimum level of receipts of £3 per week to keep any passenger station open. The doubling of the Broad Oak line up to its junction with the Blackbrook branch, and the laying in of Marsh's sidings on the same line further improved the facilities for the heavy coal traffic on that very busy branch.

*The Rainford and Eccleston Branches*

In the early fifties the St Helens Railway was very concerned about the incursions of other railways into the territory, which up to then had been its own — the rich coalbearing area around its home town. The Liverpool & Manchester Railway had been authorised to build a line to Rainford in 1845, but although two years later the local company had been empowered to lease it, nothing had ultimately materialised. In November 1851 plans for a St Helens & Southport Railway were deposited. Two separate lines were envisaged, the first running from Southport via Halsall to Ormskirk, where it would join the Liverpool-Preston line. The other was to run to Rainford from an end-on junction in Skelmersdale with the still-uncompleted East Lancashire Railway branch from Ormskirk. At Rainford, there was to be a triangular junction with the Liverpool & Bury Railway main line (by this time part of the Lancashire & Yorkshire Railway), and the projected railway would then run on to St Helens. Although the scheme quickly died, the St Helens directors were at least aware of the potential threat, as plans were being drawn up for their own line to Rainford, and these were deposited on 30 November 1852. As originally projected, this was to start from a junction with the Ravenhead branch in St Helens and, after running through the town, head northwards to pass under the L & B line at Rainford en route to its terminus at Bawdy Lane, where in due course it was hoped to make an end-on junction with the ELR Ormskirk branch. In the first draft of the scheme, it was to be 6 miles 7.86 chains in length, with gradients of 1 in 66 between Old Mill Lane and Rainford Junction, where there was to be a connection to the main line to give through running in the Wigan direction.

In was also decided to include in the Bill a short branch from near Ravenhead Copper Works to Eccleston, mainly to serve the collieries and works belonging to Samuel Taylor. This was to be 1 mile 42.50 chains in length, with a ruling gradient of 1 in 84, and would have the

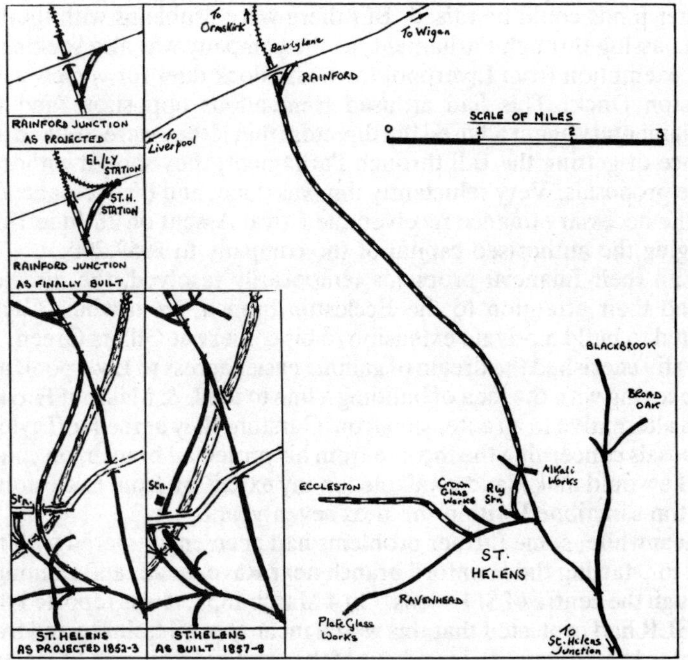


ST. HELENS RAILWAY RAINFORD & ECCLESTON BRANCH PROJECTS 1852-3.

only tunnel on the St Helens Railway System. The Bill received the Royal Assent on 4 August 1853. The cost was estimated at £93,785, but no additional capital was sought. Five years were allowed for their construction, and the Act also stipulated that the new railway should now pass over the Liverpool-Wigan line at Rainford. On the same day the ELR also obtained authority to extend its Ormskirk-Skelmersdale branch to Rainford but, despite its avowed intention of completing the line in three years, work did not start in earnest until June 1857.

The St Helens Railway, too, became involved with other matters, and nothing serious was undertaken on the Rainford and Eccleston branches until July 1856, when it was decided to give notice to the various landowners that purchase of the necessary land for both lines would soon commence. In the following month, the directors obtained sanction from the shareholders to vary the course of the line through St Helens, but they were also forced to admit the need for further capital. Indeed the contractors at work on the Rainford branch, Thornton & McCormick, were forced to accept a deferred payment in January 1856, as the company was not able to meet their stage payments until further funds could be raised. But there were problems with the Bill then passing through Parliament, as the company was also seeking to gain exemption from Liverpool town and dock dues for vessels using Garston Dock. This had aroused tremendous oppostion, and the Parliamentary agent advised the directors that if they were to stand any chance of getting the Bill through Parliament, they should withdraw these proposals. Very reluctantly this was done, and the Act sanctioning the necessary finance received the Royal Assent on 26 June 1857, bringing the authorised capital of the company to £959,200.

With their financial problems temporarily resolved, the directors turned their attention to the Eccleston branch, from which Taylor wanted to build a private extension to his colliery at Gillars Green. As they still cherished the dream of gaining easier access to Liverpool, and were toying with the idea of building a line to the L & M line at Huyton as an alternative to an extension from Garston, they agreed to Taylor's proposals concerning the income from his projected branch, on condition he would make land available for any extension from Eccleston to Huyton sanctioned within the next seven years.

Meanwhile, some further problems had been encountered with the plan for starting the Rainford branch near Ravenhead, and running it through the centre of St Helens. On 4 March 1857, it was reported that the ELR had protested that this would mean that all trains to and from Rainford had to reverse in and out of the terminal station in St Helens. Just over a month later, the board decided to purchase land between Hall Road and the canal for a new through station and goods yard on a site close to that of the present Shaw Street station. In fact, Cross had already started work on plans both for this and for alterations to the

Rainford branch, which was now to pass under instead of over Raven Street, so that with a relatively minor deviation it could link up with the original plan north of Gerard's Bridge.

Once money was available, work on the Rainford branch proceeded quickly, with up to 660 men employed on its construction. On 17 October 1857 Cross was able to report that the line had already been tested with a trial engine, and could be ready for goods traffic by 1 December. The directors inspected the line nine days later, but although they were impressed with what they saw, they decided to delay the opening until the Ormskirk-Rainford line was ready. Although Cross had provided plans and estimates for the new station early in the year. he did not receive approval for his final design until 4 December. Moreover the directors had virtually ignored the need for intermediate stations on the new line, so on 9 January 1858 they made a site visit to finalise the positions of stations at Gerard's Bridge, Moss Bank, and Rainford. At Rainford Junction the local company was to occupy a small hut on the long curving branch platform incorporated in the new station, which the L & Y was building to replace the L & B Rainford station. The St Helens Railway Rainford station, about a mile to the south, was renamed Rainford Village in November 1861, although the April 1864 working timetable still refers to it simply as Rainford. Almost as an afterthought, the company decided to site a station and a siding at Crank Lane, and a simple hut at Rookery, at which trains would be stopped experimentally to see if traffic warranted the erection of a permanent station.

Despite these last minute decisions, all the main stations were completed by a local builder, Richard Harrison, in time for the Board of Trade Inspector on 26 January 1858. The Rainford branch, and the south to east curve to the main line at Rainford Junction, were passed for traffic, and together with the new station in St Helens opened on 1 February 1858. Passenger services commenced with four trains in each direction, connecting with Liverpool and Wigan trains at Rainford Junction. Despite repeated exhortations over the previous few months, the ELR line was not ready, and this, together with the north to east curve at Rainford Junction, built without specific statutory authority, were not opened for traffic until 1 March 1858. The stations at Rookery and Crank did not open until towards the end of 1858, and the former was closed in March 1862. It was replaced on 1 June 1865 by a new station bearing the same name, but some fifty chains to the north.

The contract for the Eccleston branch had been awarded to a Mr Knight for £7368 and work proceeded steadily, with up to 160 men employed at peak periods. On 1 March 1859 a trial engine conveyed Cross and Knight on an inspection of the line to Gillars Green Colliery, and as the line was intended solely for freight traffic, there was no delay in its opening. But all was not well, and on 26 March a report in the 'St Helens Intelligencer' adds a touch of unintentional humour . . . "Owing to the heavy rains of last week a portion of the tunnel at Cropper Hill over the Eccleston Branch railway just completed, fell in. The damage, which will be considerable, will, it is stated, fall upon Mr Knight, the Contractor."

These were the last major lines built by the St Helens Railway before the end of its independent existence. Statistics for the end of June 1858 show that in a little over ten years its workforce had grown almost sixfold to a total of 647, excluding anyone at work on the Eccleston branch. It had some 31 miles of line open to traffic, and its passenger stations had increased to 21, compared with the four open in 1848.

*Relationship with the LNWR*

We must now step back a few years to review the comany's increasing involvement with the LNWR, which in the first instance appeared to be to the advantage of the St Helens Railway. The relationship really existed on two levels, for behind the relatively friendly cooperation in day-to-day affairs lay the cut and thrust of high level politics, as other railway companies entered the arena, and battles raged over the creation of the second southern route between Liverpool and Manchester, and an improved route between Merseyside and London.

On 18 August 1851, having heard that the LNWR was proposing to build a line in Liverpool from Edge Hill to the Dingle, the St Helens directors instructed Rendel to draw up a new plan for a Liverpool extension in conjunction with Nathaniel Beardmore, who had collaborated in the 1847 scheme. But after a meeting of singular duplicity in Liverpool, both companies announced their intention to abstain from proposing or supporting in the current Parliamentary session, any line which might affect the other company either west of Garston, between the L & M line and the Mersey, or between St Helens and Huyton. Such a statement was totally meaningless, as the local company still intended to reach Liverpool, while, despite its avowed "pacifist policy and friendly understanding", the LNWR really saw no point in putting off its plans while moving towards a "more extended and comprehensive alliance" as a prelude to the absorption of the St Helens Railway. Although its directors were too wary to fall into the trap, and the LNWR had to wait for almost ten years before the first fatal steps were taken, the two companies did really seem on the verge of a very close liaison, for the board of minutes of 20 October 1851 contain a Memorandum of Agreement to be signed between them. This confirmed that the LNWR was not to make any lines within the St Helens Railway sphere of operations without the consent of the local company, and also specifically stated that "The St Helens Railway is not to make any extensions to Liverpool." The LNWR guaranteed a minimum shipment of 160,000 tons of coal a year through Garston Dock three years after its opening, with compensation for the local company if this was not achieved. In return the St Helens Railway had to route traffic from Garston to destinations beyond Warrington over the LNWR rather than over the Warrington & Altrincham line. To facilitate this traffic, a connection was to be laid in at Bank Quay to connect the west coast main line to the St Helens Railway Warrington branch, while the St Helens Railway was to provide a south to east connection at St Helens Junction and lay in sidings to facilitate exchange of traffic. Neither connection was ever built, but the St Helens Railway purchased fourteen acres for improvements at St Helens Junction, and in due course used some of the land for its new sheds and workshops.

The Agreement was signed and sealed by both companies on 5 November 1851 but the solemn undertakings did not inhibit the St Helens directors from instructing Beardmore to complete plans for the Liverpool extension. But there was a natural reluctance to have a head-on clash with the LNWR, so nothing was proposed for the 1853 Parliamentary session. Discussions took place in the following year about a joint line to Liverpool, but without result, and so the local company indicated that it would carry on alone. In the event no plans were put forward for the 1855 session, but some acrimony was caused when in November 1854 a rival scheme for a Liverpool & Garston railway was deposited bearing the names of Vignoles and Beardmore. As these worthies were both associated with the St Helens Railway the LNWR required some persuading that this was not a secret move by the local company. Still, in the following year both companies affected surprise when the North Staffordshire Railway deposited plans for a line from Garston to Liverpool for the 1856 Parliamentary session. The St Helens Railway was not happy with some of the proposals, for in addition to requesting running powers over the St Helens and W & S Railways, the NSR also sought sanction to lease, buy or amalgamate with one or both of the local lines. The LNWR was again suspicious, as these plans bore the names of Beardmore and Rendel. so both companies were a little relieved when the NSR bill was withdrawn in March 1856, although some attempts were made to revive the scheme in the following year.

*The End of the Warrington & Stockport Railway*

As we have already seen the MS & L was also interested in gaining access to Liverpool. As one of the partners in the MSJA, and now working the W & S, it was ideally placed to make such a move in conjunction with the St Helens Railway. The W & S was by this time almost bankrupt, and as recounted at the half yearly meeting in August 1857, had only been kept going by a £15,000 loan from its directors.

The Chairman, W C Fosbery, explained that the company now intended to apply for powers to raise £33,286, which together with unissued stock of £20,490, would legally provide for all existing unsecured loans and liabilities.

Thus the company was ripe for takeover, and the St Helens board minutes for 17 October 1857 indicate that the MS & L had suggested a joint leasing of the line, with the local company taking a one third share. This proposition had also been discussed with the LNWR at a meeting in Liverpool, so that the latter could participate if it so wished. Closer links with the MS & L were already forged, as the St Helens Railway had just agreed to full running powers for the MS & L and GN Railways between Warrington and Garston. The board had also decided to back the MS & L scheme for a line from Garston to Liverpool, which it proposed to build at a cost of £140,000. On 20 January 1858 the MS & L made public its proposals to construct this line in conjunction with the St Helens and Great Northern Railways, together with a lease of the W & S, and an undertaking to carry out that company's now abandoned Stockport extension. To gain public support, a through service of two trains a day beetween Kings Cross and Garston was introduced on 1 February 1858, with express omnibuses taking passengers to and from the GN offices in Liverpool. The W & S then decided to exercise its running powers over the BLCJ line, as defined in the Act of 20 August 1853, and introduced a connecting service from Chester to Warrington. But on 1 March 1858, when the W & S trains was waiting at Chester, the BLCJ officials took matters into their own hands and removed a rail, effectively imprisoning the train for half an hour. In due course, the LNWR obtained a court order restraining the MS & L and W & S from using Chester station, but the W & S was allowed to continue its Chester services while litigation continued, although these were discontinued on 1 September 1858, because of the intransigent attitude of the BLCJ.

Meanwhile, the W & S Leasing Bill was presented to Parliament in the 1858 session by the MS & L and St Helens Railways, for although the GN like the LNW had been approached, it had not taken up any options to participate. The Bill guaranteed the W & S shareholders a 3½ per cent return in the first year, rising to 5 per cent in the fourth year and thereafter. Despite the strenuous opposition of the LNWR, the Bill passed the Commons with the period of the lease reduced from 999 years to 10 years, but it was rejected by the Lords at the end of July 1858. The Bill for the Garston & Liverpool Railway was also rejected on the grounds that the capital had not actually been raised. Unabashed, Watkin put forward a new scheme in the next session, although at £450,000 this was three times the cost of the previous proposal, with the St Helens Railway contribution fixed at one fifth, and that of the MS & L and GN at two fifths each.

All this had not stopped the St Helens Railway from submitting its own plan for a Garston-Liverpool line, which had been drawn up by James Cross for the 1858 Parliamentary session. It proposed a main line just over 3 miles 5 furlongs long, terminating at Beresford Road in Liverpool, together with a branch 2½ furlongs long into the southern docks. This joined the internal dock railway system approximately where the CLC Brunswick station was ultimately built. The hearing before the House of Commons Committee opened on 1 June 1858, and there were many stirring speeches for and against the proposal, including an accusation by the LNWR that the St Helens Railway was breaking the 1851 Agreement. After eleven days of discussion and argument, the Committee Chairman announced that the preamble to the Bill was not proven, so on 18 June 1858 the scheme was officially dead. By this time the local company had spent £3,682 12s 1d on various schemes for a line to Liverpool, and had achieved nothing. Although the St Helens Railway never again submitted a scheme of its own, it was involved to a greater or lesser extent in several abortive proposals, before the Garston & Liverpool Railway was authorised in 1861.

Meanwhile, as the demise of the W & S was now merely a matter of time, its directors had determined that it should be handed over in good order, and its financial affairs were regulated by the Act of 2 August 1858. The shareholders received a 3½% dividend for the half year ending 30 June, which seemed to take them by surprise, although this had been guaranteed by the MS & L and St Helens Railways in anticipation of the authorisation of the leasing arrangements. The Bill for the leasing of the W & S was resubmitted for the 1859 Parliamentary session. It had its second reading on 14 February 1859, and even though eleven days later the St Helens directors were still stressing their intention of proceeding with the MS & L, the option to replace the latter by the LNWR had already been inserted, and the change all but made. This was announced at a meeting of the W & S shareholders on 1 March. Stormy scenes followed, and abuse was hurled on all sides, particularly in view of the fact that the LNWR had insisted on a lower dividend level. The Bill in its amended form received the Royal Assent on 13 August 1859, and authorised the LNW and St Helens Railways to lease the W & S line for 999 years with a guaranteed dividend of 4¼ per cent. The former had a two thirds share in the enterprise, with an option to purchase the line before 1 January 1861.

At least on the surface, it seemed that relationships between the MS & L and LNW Railways were at last improving, and when on 21 July 1859 the latter obtained sanction for a line from Garston to Edge Hill in Liverpool, the MS & L thought that this might serve just as well as an independent terminus in the Merseyside city. The St Helens Railway would then be hemmed in at both ends by its powerful neighbour, and the rumour spread that the LNWR might very well lease the Garston-Warrington line. In December 1860 the LNWR exercised its option to purchase the W & S, after the St Helens Railway had finally given its consent to the sale, which took effect from 1 January 1861. The dissolution of the W & S was formalised by the LNWR (New Works and Additional Powers) Act of 15 July 1867, and so the Warrington & Stockport Railway passed into history. It had been a mere pawn in the railway wars of the 1850s, as despite a reasonable level of local traffic, its strategic importance lay as a link in the through route between the cities of Lancashire. The LNWR merely wanted possession to protect its interests, and after it had swallowed up the W & S, a fair proportion of the freight traffic passing along it was diverted to other routes.

*The Last Years of Independence*

Even before the joint leasing of the W & S was finalised, the stage was being set for the gradual absorption of the local company. At the AGM on 25 February 1859, the directors gave details of a scheme by which the LNWR would take a lease of the Garston-Warrington line for the following guaranteed payments: £9,000 in 1859, £10,000 in 1860 and £12,000 thereafter. Nothing came of this immediately, but the details were thrashed out for the 1860 Parliamentary session, and the London & North Western and St Helens Railway Companies Arrangements Act received the Royal Assent on 14 June 1860. Under the terms of the lease, the LNWR, in addition to working the line, was to be allowed free access to Garston Dock, where certain sections of the sidings and coal yards were to be reserved for its exclusive use, a levy of 3d per ton being made for dockage and tolls. These provisions came into effect from 1 July 1860, from which date the LNWR also had free access to stations at Garston and Warrington, as well as to all intermediate stations. The report of the AGM in February 1861, however, stated that the LNWR took possession of the line on 1 September 1860, and for these privileges it was to pay the local company an annual rent of £5,000 in 1860, and £12,000 in succeeding years. The local company had free use of the leased railway to carry passengers to and from Runcorn Gap, and could carry up to 250,000 tons of coal per year over the line to Garston, but 3d per ton was chargeable for any quantity above that figure. Although at first sight the financial arrangements detailed in the schedule to the Act appear favourable to the St Helens Railway, they were of much less importance to the LNWR than the control it had gained over the approaches to Liverpool and the docks.

The 1860 Act also gave the St Helens Railway authority to raise a further £100,000 in £20 shares, as well as up to £33,000 in loans. This brought the authorised capital of the company (excluding loans) to just over £1 million. Its annual turnover was now in excess of the £100,000 forecast earlier, but when working expenses, interest on loans, and dividends were deducted, only negligible amounts were being added to the reserves. Nevertheless, the directors were still involved in new projects, the most tangible of which was the provision of a new dock at West Bank, Widnes, to serve the factories now being built in that area. When opened in 1862, rail access to the dock was provided by the lines of John Hutchinson, who was building a considerable industrial estate in the area, but there was no direct access from the canal.

In September 1860 Cross was instructed to provide plans for yet another station in St Helens, as the 1858 structure was now described as 'temporary'. When the directors saw the cost estimates, it quickly became permanent, at least for another ten years. Traffic was still increasing, and in the same year some seven miles of new sidings were installed, while nine miles of the main line were relaid with heavier rail, which together with improved signalling, new walls and fences, took their toll of the company finances. The doubling of the Blackbrook branch was approved in June 1861, and a new engine shed at Garston was sanctioned at a cost of £178.

By now, with shares fully paid up and major construction completed, the financial position of the St Helens Railway should have been reasonably healthy, but dividends and interest payments literally devoured any operating surplus, and the company was running on a perpetual overdraft of between £10,000 and £12,000. In fact, the company was only kept viable by the canal, as the deficit from railway operations had not fallen below £6,000 in the previous decade, and had reached as much as £12,039 in 1855.

Construction of the LNWR Edge Hill-Garston line was now well under way, and in September 1862 Cross inspected the junction between this and the St Helens Railway and reported his satisfaction with it. Now that the Garston & Liverpool Railway had also been authorised, joint operation of Garston station with the LNW, GN and MS & L railways would be necessary, and an agreement for this purpose was concluded on 9 July 1863. Meanwhile, on 11 July 1861 the LNWR had been authorised to construct a line from Acton Bridge on its west coast main line, which would cross the Mersey at Runcorn and join the St Helens Railway near Ditton to give a new and improved route from Merseyside to London.

Although the LNWR had already leased the section of line needed for this route, the total acquisition of the local company had become of paramount importance. One of the reasons for this is given by Baines in his "History of Lancashire", where he stated that "the St Helens line which forms only one fortieth of the London and North Western Company's mileage, conveys an annual 2,000,000 tons of minerals and goods or one seventh of their entire merchandise traffic". This is amply borne out by official returns, as in 1863 the railway (excluding any traffic confined to Warrington-Garston section) carried 1,357,704 tons against 6,118,611 tons on the whole of the LNWR system in the same period. Despite their wish to remain independent, the inevitability of a takeover was now apparent to the St Helens Railway directors, and they had no choice but to secure the best possible terms for such an amalgamation.

In October 1863 serious discussions began on the transfer of the St Helens Railway to the LNWR and LYR jointly, or to either one of them from 1 July 1864, but the Bill deposited on 24 December 1863 was specifically for a transfer to the LNWR. Public concern was great, and a committee was set up to ensure that the interests of the locality were safeguarded. The Committee succeeded in getting a clause inserted in the Transfer Bill, which prevented any increase in the maximum charges on the canal, so that they would not be entirely at the mercy of the railway company. The Bill also sought to guarantee the continuance of the clauses in the London & North Western Railway (Lines near Liverpool) Act of 1861 which safeguarded the entrance to Widnes Dock and the Sankey Canal, both during and after the building of the Runcorn Bridge authorised by it.

The committee stage of the Transfer Bill commenced on 4 June 1864, and local industrial interests were well represented with a remit to secure the reduction of tolls on the railway, the assignment of running powers into St Helens to the LYR, and the improvement of the crossing of the Garston and St Helens lines in Widnes. They also wanted the depth of water in the canal to be increased from 5ft 9in to 6ft 3in to facilitate the passage of larger boats, as well as the repeal of the provisions of the 1845 Act of Amalgamation, which allowed the company to close unprofitable sections of the waterway.

Much of the evidence submitted stressed the desirability of the link with the LNWR. In the previous six months no less than 72,102 tons of coal had passed to and from the LNWR compared with a mere 10,006 tons to and from the LYR. These points were given added emphasis by the LNWR Traffic Manager, who stated that amalgamation was essential, if much needed improvements to the track and facilities on the Warrington and Garston lines and at the docks were to be carried out, so that the continuing increase in traffic could be efficiently handled.

The St Helens Canal & Railway Transfer Act of 29 July 1864 authorised the absorption of the local company by the LNWR, who guaranteed a dividend on the ordinary stock of 4 per cent in 1865, 4½ per cent in 1866 and 5 per cent thereafter. At the time of the amalgamation the whole of the authorised capital of £1,059,200 had been subscribed, and all except £6 of the loans had been raised, giving a total of £1,412,214, almost ten times the amount sanctioned by the 1830 Act, when the company had come into being.

It had already been announced at a Special General Meeting of the St Helens Railway shareholders on 22 June 1864, that the transfer to

*Liverpool & Manchester Railway Viaduct over the Sankey Navigation Canal, from a print by T Bury (Science Museum, London).*

*Vertical-boiler Locomotive on St Helens & Runcorn Gap Railway, crossing Liverpool & Manchester Railway near the foot of Sutton Incline, from a print by T Bury (Science Museum, London).*

*Seal of the St Helens Canal & Railway Company 1845 (National Railway Museum)*

*Charles Blacker Vignoles (1793-1875) as a young man (St Helens Library)*

*Top: drawing of St Helens Railway 0-4-0 No 1 'Navvie' produced by Edward Borrows for its rebuilding in 1857 (St Helens Library)*

*Centre: St Helens Railway 0-4-2 No 4 'Hercules', as built in 1856. 'Hercules' was rebuilt as a tank engine prior to 1861 (St Helens Library)*

*Bottom: St Helens Railway 2-4-0 No 9 'Swallow' (St Helens Library)*

St Helens Railway 2-4-2 tank No 21 'Raven' as originally built — shown in white livery about 1863 outside Sutton Works (St Helens Library)

St Helens Railway 0-4-2 No 26 'Clyde' (St Helens Library)

*Coal tipplers in action on a wet day at the Old Dock, Garston, on 1 December 1976 (J M Tolson)*

*Ex LMSR 2-6-2 tank 41211 at Ditton Junction with the 4.19 pm motor train from Manchester Oxford Road on 1 September 1962. The station was totally rebuilt for the electrification of the Liverpool-Crewe line (J M Tolson)*

*Remains of the St Helens Railway West Bank Dock at Widnes on 10 April 1976. Runcorn can be seen in the background together with the railway bridge across the Mersey, completed by the LNWR in 1868, and the road bridge opened in 1961. (J M Tolson)*

*Remains of a swivel bridge which once carried the St Helens Railway line over the Sankey Canal at Widnes. Part of the original mechanism in the foreground bears the inscription 'Haigh Iron Works 1832'. The view looking over the site of the sidings adjacent to the railway dock was taken in November 1970. (J M Tolson)*

*The flat crossing of the Widnes-St Helens and Warrington-Garston lines in Widnes looking towards Ditton. BR standard 2-6-0 No 76077 heads the LCGB 'Warrington and Widnes Brake Van' Railtour past Widnes No 4 Box on 5 August 1967. (J M Tolson)*

*Main buildings at Warrington Arpley, once the headquarters of the Warrington & Stockport Railway, looking towards the bridge over the Mersey — taken on 5 February 1966. (J M Tolson)*

*Ex LMSR 'Jubilee' Class 4-6-0 45581 'Bihar and Orissa' heads a train of empty coal waggons through Appleton as it climbs towards St Helens. Appleton station was closed from 18 June 1951, but some of the buildings were still standing when this view was taken on 10 January 1962 (J M Tolson)*

*Ex LMSR Class 8F 2-8-0 48249 heads the daily Old Fold (Haydock Junction)-Canada Dock coal train past the northern connection to Sutton Manor Colliery on the St Helens-Widnes line — 2 March 1962 (J M Tolson)*

*Crowds waiting to see the Royal Train at St Helens Junction. A Webb Compound 2-2-2-0 (probably No. 507 'Marchioness of Stafford') is on empty stock, while a DX class 0-6-0 pauses on the former St Helens Railway line. This view was taken some time in the 1880s, approximately from the same place as the Bury print, and shows that the original bridge has been removed and replaced by a more utilitarian structure. (St Helens Library)*

*Webb 2-4-2 tank No 6628 was still in LMS livery when photographed at Sutton Oak on a typical motor train working on 26 April 1951 (H C Casserley)*

*St Helens station looking towards Liverpool with a Wigan-Liverpool dmu about to depart on 7 August 1972 (J M Tolson)*

*Ex LMSR 'Jubilee' Class 4-6-0 45570 'New Zealand' shunting near St Helens goods station on 4 May 1962 (J M Tolson)*

*Pilkington Brothers 0-4-0 well tank 'Briars Hey' built by Edward Borrows & Sons (Works No 52/1908) attacks a steep bank near Gerard's Bridge, St Helens, on 10 August 1958 (J Peden)*

*Pilkington Brothers 0-4-0 diesel hydraulic (Yorkshire Engine 2820/1961) DH2 heads a train of empty trucks past a heap of sand on the internal rail system near Ravenhead Junction. In the background are the St Helens Canal and the St Helens-Huyton line in this view taken on 7 August 1972 (J M Tolson)*

*Remains of Winwick Lock and lockkeeper's cottage on the St Helens Canal — 24 April 1971 (J M Tolson)*

*The head of the Blackbrook branch of the St Helens Canal, now a placid pool, but once very busy with the coal traffic brought to it by a number of tramways; 7 August 1972. (J M Tolson)*

the LNWR would take place on 31 July on the agreed terms. The report of the meeting in the 'St Helens Newspaper & Advertiser' aptly summed up the general feeling: "The Chairman . . . said that they might congratulate themselves on having done well. The transfer was a very good bargain for them, and not a very bad one for the London & North Western Railway Company."

On 29 July 1864 the directors and some senior officials of the LNWR visited the St Helens Railway in a special train hauled by the engine 'Carlisle', to inspect the various stations and facilities, before formally taking possession on 1 August. They had a good lunch at the Raven Hotel and went home well pleased.

## CHAPTER VI

# INTERLUDE — A TRANSPORT MONOPOLY

With all the frenzied activity on the railway after 1845, it was only natural that the canal should fade a little into the background. Canal-borne traffic still benefited under the terms of the 1762 and 1830 Acts, in which the maximum tariff for the whole length of the waterway from St Helens to Runcorn Gap had been fixed at 1s 0d per long ton. Although important traffic such as copper ore and salt had enjoyed the same terms as for coal, this had been merely custom and practice, as no specific provision had been made for these in the original acts. No change was made in 1830, and in the 1845 Act of Amalgamation the various industrialists also missed their chance to get statutory limitations on the rate charged for those commodities. As the imperial ton of 20 cwt was now in more general use, and indeed expressly stipulated in the 1846 Act for the Garston extension, the directors of the combined enterprise decided to use this measurement for all items, where they were not legally bound to use the long ton. This gave scope for a 50 per cent increase on salt, pyrites and other raw materials for the glass, copper and alkali industries, if these were carried on the canal. Although the rates then in force were only 8d per ton, due to the fierce price cutting of the pre-amalgamation years, these were raised by a penny in July 1848, and then to the maximum of 1s 0d for pyrites in October 1854, followed by copper ore and all other up traffic from 19 January 1855.

A charge was made on the railway for the carriage of lime, limestone and manure, traditionally carried toll free on the waterway, and as the majority of coal traffic was carried in the collieries' own waggons, the effective difference in carriage rates between coal and items such as salt and mineral ores even in 1846 was 1½d per ton per mile. This was quite a considerable sum, as 10-12 tons of raw material were required to produce one ton of soda by the Leblanc process, and 40-50 tons of ore only made one ton of cake copper. Costs for the alkali makers and copper smelters were not helped when the basic rail carriage rates between Runcorn Gap and St Helens were increased to 1s 6d per ton in 1848, 1s 9d per ton in 1854 and 2s 0d in 1859, by which time the rate between Garston and St Helens had reached 2s 6d per ton. Conversely the tariff for carrying coal between St Helens and Garston was reduced to 1s 5d per ton on 20 October 1854, so a move away from St Helens was obviously attractive to alkali manufacturers. At Runcorn Gap in particular, there would be far less claims from outraged landowners, as the prevailing wind blew over the largely uninhabited marshes, where the evil-smelling waste could also be dumped well away from human habitation. The increase in coal traffic rates between St Helens and Garston to 1s 9d in October 1858, was really no deterrent, so by making St Helens less attractive to the chemical industry, the St Helens Railway helped to stimulate the phenomenal growth of industrial Widnes.

Carriage rates were not the only source of annoyance in St Helens, where the railway was continually criticised for its general attitude to customers, and the havoc it caused when crossing public roads. The 'St Helens Newspaper & Advertiser' for 30 June 1863, has a more than usually vitriolic editorial comment: "The fares, both for passengers and merchandise, have from time to time been raised, and every conceivable obstacle and annoyance has been resorted to, and perseveringly practised, until there is scarcely a single tradesman or manufacturer but has his grievance to complain of, and who heartily wishes that the present company was defunct and the line transferred to other hands, or, that some other company would construct another and a rival line to meet the growing wants of the town and district. To such an extent has the nuisance grown that manufacturers are seriously conceiving the idea of transferring their works to Widnes and elsewhere . . . In addition to its being the worst line in the kingdom to travel over, it *excels* all others, with which we are acquainted, in uncertainty as to time and charges and want of accommodation . . . The reckless and spendthrift policy of the Railway Company shows itself in almost every act connected with its daily operation and management."

Such was the view widely held by local industrialists in a town whose population was to grow to 45,266 by 1871. But before the final swingeing increases in transport rates took effect, chemical manufacturers still found it worthwhile to come to St Helens, although only one copper smelting or alkali company started up in the town after 1854. Public outcry against pollution ultimately bore fruit in the Alkali Works Regulation Act of 28 July 1863, so that from 1 January of the following year, 95 per cent of all hydrochloric acid vapour had to be condensed, a move which had cost the industry over £200,000 by the time a Royal Commission investigated the same problem in 1878. Moreover the waste disposal problems for the alkali industry waste were enormous, as many thousands of tons were involved each year, and manufacturers were often in confrontation with the St Helens Railway for polluting the canal.

The glass trade made major expansions and technological advances during the middle years of the nineteenth century, and the repeal of the window tax in 1851 enabled Pilkingtons to almost double its output of window glass between 1850 and 1854. But the mighty Ravenhead Plate Works fell on hard times and was taken over by the Liverpool & Manchester Plate Glass Works, whose works near the railway at Sutton Oak was claimed to be the largest in the country in 1855. In 1867 William Pilkington said that the town made two thirds of the country's plate glass, one third of its window glass, and about one tenth of its bottle and flint glass, which he rather optimistically estimated at about half the total output of glass in Britain.

The move of industry to Widnes, which even in 1841 was a scattered and largely rural community of only 2,209 inhabitants, was really set in motion by John Hutchinson, who, having worked at Kurtz's Alkali Works in St Helens, built his first factory in Widnes in 1847 on a strip of land between the canal and the railway dock. In due course he created a considerable private railway system, and the first privately-owned locomotive in the town was built for this by Thomas Robinson at the Widnes Foundry. Some well known figures in the chemical industry, such as William Gossage and Frederick Muspratt, came to Widnes relatively early, but the main exodus of chemical manufacturers from St Helens took place after the second major increase of tolls and charges in 1854.

The industry thus created had an almost insatiable need for coal, and coal-mining flourished in St Helens, with even Pilkington Brothers becoming involved in it. Factories in Widnes alone were taking 120,000 tons a year by rail and canal by 1863, although this was still only about half as much as that passing down the canal to the salt works. In 1863 coal consumption in St Helens was around 700,000 tons, but in the Alkali Inspector's Report for 1868 the estimate had risen to one million tons, and two years later Kurtz's Alkali Works alone was recorded as having an annual consumption of 62,400 tons.

Meanwhile by 1865, the year in which John Hutchinson died, the population of Widnes had reached 10,000, but its industries were expanding at such a phenomenal rate that sixteen years later this had increased to 24,935. By then Widnes was well on the way to becoming what a writer in the 'Daily News' of 1881 described as "the dirtiest, ugliest and most depressing town in England".

## CHAPTER VII
# LOCOMOTIVES

The first specific mention of a locomotive for use on the St Helens Railway appeared in the board minutes for 17 November 1831, when Vignoles was requested to ascertain the cost of hiring an engine from the L & M to work the section of line from St Helens to the junction, which was then nearing completion. It was later recorded that the L & M were willing to hire *North Star* at a cost of £20 per month including crew. Both this engine and *Majestic* certainly worked on the local line towards the end of 1831, but the locomotive actually used for the official opening of the line on 2 January 1832, was No 14 *Jupiter*.

At the end of March 1832 a specification for locomotive engines was detailed in the minutes: "The wheels to be 54 inches Diameter, Axles 5 inches, Diameter Cylinders 13 inches, Stroke 20 inches, Weight with water in the Boiler not to exceed 8 tons; the engine to work with coal, and the four wheels to be moved, the Boiler guaranteed to generate steam to a power of not less than 2,500 lbs at a velocity of 10 miles per hour giving a capability of the engine of drawing 150 tons, including its own weight and that of the tender, at a rate of 5 miles per hour up an inclination of 1 in 400."

It was decided to purchase three locomotives from the Horseley Iron Company of Tipton for £450 each; delivery of the first locomotive was requested by 1 August 1832, and all were in service by the opening of the main line in February 1833. Although future comments were to indicate dissatisfaction with the original locomotives, the decision to order a fourth from the Horseley Iron Company for £600 was taken in April 1833. This engine was somewhat of a mystery, although the L & M were sufficiently impressed by a trial held on the St Helens Railway on 31 October 1833 to order the 2-2-0 *Star* from the same company. Three further locomotives with 4ft 6in wrought iron wheels and 12in x 18in cylinders were ordered in May 1833 for £900 each from Edward Bury of Liverpool for delivery within six months. Only two tenders were ordered from Bury, the third coming from Galloway & Bowman for £120.

The celebrated Braithwaite & Ericsson locomotive *Novelty* also spent some time on the local line, mainly on construction trains, and in August 1833 it was recorded in Rastrick's 'Rainhill Notebook' that it was fitted with a new copper tubular boiler by Daglish, who was responsible for the preservation of the original cylinders for posterity. Two other vertical boiler locomotives, *King William IV* and *Queen Adelaide* also saw service on the St Helens Railway, and it is probably one of these which appears in the well known Ackermann print of the intersection bridge over the L & M at St Helens Junction.

Delivery of the Bury locomotives, of which the first was named *Widnes*, was completed in the first half of 1834. In May of the same year, the company also purchased the locomotive *Viaduct*, built by Jones & Company of the Viaduct Foundry, Newton-le-Willows, from one of its own directors for £700.

On 10 August 1835 it was decided to dispose of the first two Horseley locomotives *Greenall* and *St Helens*, together with 'sundry old iron and other effects not in use'. These were almost certainly the two locomotives advertised in the 'Leeds Mercury' in September and October, but their ultimate fate is not known. The wisdom of this sale may be doubted, as the company was continually under fire for its failure to deal with increasing traffic. Matters came to a head in April 1836, when it was discovered that Jones was about to sell elsewhere two locomotives he was building, although he had promised one to the company. To mollify the directors, he let them have the engine *Collier*, which had been supplied to Bournes & Robinson in October 1832, for use at their Elton Head Colliery, but this was obviously no bargain. Jones did not deliver the new engine he had promised until shortly before the expiry of his contract to operate the railway in December 1837. At that point the valuation of the company motive power was given as £6,727 5s 0½d, just over £1,000 up on the 1834 valuation.

Meanwhile the new Superintendent, Thomas Lunt, who had been appointed in November 1837, had produced a specification for locomotive power. Engines were to have 12½in x 18in cylinders with single slide valves, and metallic spring pistons with a cast steel piston rod. Each was to be provided with four 5ft coupled wheels, a boiler 3ft 4in in diameter and a copper firebox. The outside frames were 'to be well seasoned oak 3in thick and 7in deep, cased on both sides with best ¾in plates.' The Haigh Foundry of Wigan quoted £1,385 for such a locomotive, with delivery of the first in five months, and the second to follow six weeks later. On 20 November 1837 the directors decided to purchase two.

The crank axle on the new engine *Sutton*, supplied by Jones, sheared on 28 February 1838, and the company were offered a choice of one of the locomotives being built at the Viaduct Foundry at a price of £1,300 for a six-wheeler or £1,100 for the four-wheel version. The directors chose the latter. This engine, *Parr*, had 4ft 6in driving wheels and 13in x 20in cylinders.

In October 1838, Lunt reported favourably on the two engines from the Haigh Foundry, *St Helens* and *Runcorn*, but the next specific mention of a locomotive was almost exactly a year later, when it was recorded that Kirtley & Co of Warrington were to make a firebox for an engine called *Director*, but although this was apparently built in 1834, it is not certain from which builder it came.

Despite additions to stock and the repeated assurances given by Peter Greenall at successive meetings of the shareholders, the industrialists and mineowners in the area continued to complain about lack of motive power, which was not helped by long delays in carrying out repairs to *Parr* and *Viaduct*.

An engine fell in the canal near Pocket Nook on 8 January 1842, as the swing bridge had been left open at that point in accordance with operating instructions. No further details are available, but the 'Railway Times' was of the opinion that it would have to be dismantled, as no suitable tackle was available to lift it. On 14 April 1843 Daglish complained to the directors about the condition of the locomotive *Mersey*, which he said was totally unfit for traffic. He requested permission to write it off or cannibalise it. Whether this happened is not known, as on 12 May 1851 a locomotive named *Mersey* was involved in an accident, but it is more likely that this was the locomotive *Thalaba* purchased from the LNWR in the previous month.

In an Appendix to the Gauge Commissioners Report of 1846, based on material supplied in August 1845, we get details of the nine locomotives then owned by the St Helens Railway, which were all said to be four wheeled with inside cylinders:

| | |
|---|---|
| 1 with driving wheels 4ft 0in | Cylinders 14 in x 22in |
| 1 with driving wheels 4ft 4in | Cylinders 12¾in x 18in |
| 1 with driving wheels 4ft 6in | Cylinders 10 in x 16in |
| 4 with driving wheels 4ft 6in | Cylinders 12 in x 18in |
| 1 with driving wheels 4ft 6in | Cylinders 13 in x 20in |
| 1 with driving wheels 5ft 0in | Cylinders 13 in x 18in |

It is interesting to speculate on the identity of these locomotives, but it is not possible to formulate with any accuracy a detailed stock list at this date. One thing is certain — they were all of limited power, and it was said that a strong head wind had a terrible effect on their ability to start their train. In fact, in the early days, when an engine was in trouble on a steepish gradient, it was reputedly the custom for the guard to call to the people in the open thirds — 'Come on lads, lend a hand to give a shove to the train just to start the engine.'

After the amalgamation the St Helens Railway generally moved away from purchasing new engines to buying second hand items, mainly from the LNWR, but identities are not easy to determine, and their lives were relatively short.

Nine locomotives with the following names were working the railway about 1849:

| | | |
|---|---|---|
| *Runcorn* | *Widnes* | *Eagle* |
| *St Helens* | *Director* | *Blackbrook* |
| *John Smith* | *Navvie* | *Swan* |

*Blackbrook* was almost certainly a new engine in that year, while a local historian writing in the 1890s stated that *Director* was probably used to haul the first train for the opening of the new St Helens station in December 1849, but no other evidence has been found to substantiate this.

After the opening of this station and the levelling of the inclined planes, the directors made real efforts to cater for passenger traffic, and in May 1850 they purchased one of 'Messrs Adam's Patent Steam Carriages' capable of carrying 100 passengers, for £1,760. Whether this was successful is not known, but the power unit survived as the 2-2-0 tank *Resurgam*.

Despite the increasing number of locomotives, the railway was still not always able to cope with heavy traffic, and mine owners often made application to run their own locomotives over the company's tracks. While this was to some extent allowed on the branches, the directors generally would not sanction it on the main line, for they had enough troubles keeping control of their own train crews, despite a spate of regulations governing their conduct.

Nevertheless the directors were concerned about the problem, and in March 1850 bought the LNWR 'Bird' class locomotive No 128 *Swallow*, which had begun life in 1840 as a 2-2-2, but by January 1855 had become a 2-4-0, and underwent a further rebuilding in this form in 1857.

In April 1851 the company bought two more LNWR engines, the 0-4-2 No 70 *Sphinx* and the 2-2-2 No 36 *Thalaba* for £900. The next purchases came in February 1852, when the company bought the 2-2-2 No 147 *Woodlark* and the 0-4-2 No 142 *Atlas* for £860. This was closely followed by the purchase of No 1 *Saracen* and No 7 *Scorpion*, sister engines of *Sphinx*, and dating from 1842, for £1,135, although only one tender was included in the deal. In December 1852 the 2-4-0 No 142 *Bittern* was purchased for £450, and no further acquisitions are mentioned in company minute books for several years. *Sphinx, Saracen* and *Scorpion* retained their own names after purchase, but *Thalaba* and *Woodlark* became *Mersey* and *Star* in the local company's stock. It is likely, too, that *Atlas* and *Bittern* were renamed *Sutton* and *Britain* respectively, but this has not been confirmed.

A survey taken early in 1853 indicated that the existing locomotive stock would be sufficient to cope with all traffic emanating from the impending opening of Garston Dock. But, as the locomotive stock of the company more than doubled from twelve in June 1851 to 25 in January 1855, not including a new engine under construction, the progress of acquisition must be sought elsewhere.

The sale of No 125 *Soho* to Robert Daglish was recorded by the LNWR in 1852, and it is possible that this was rebuilt by him and sold to the St Helens Railway to become the engine *Garston*. The 2-2-2 tank *Queen*, built by Fairbairn for the Great Exhibition at the Crystal Palace in 1851, was certainly on the St Helens Railway in 1853, as a note dated 27 April lists the passenger locomotives as *Mersey, Navvy, Woodlark, Swallow, Queen*, and *Resurgam*. A further 'Bird' class 2-4-0 No 143 *Lapwing* was obtained from the LNWR in September 1853, and the probability exists that a further five 'Bird' class engines may have found their way on to the local system in the following two years.

Two new locomotives, both 0-4-2, *Hero* and *Goliath*, were built by the St Helens Railway in 1853 and 1854, and the locomotive *Alma* mentioned in a list dated January 1855, was probably a rebuild of an unidentified 'Bird' class engine.

On 30 June 1854, the valuation of the company rolling stock including locomotives, carriages and waggons was £48,835 6s 0d, but a further assessment in January 1855 is particularly valuable, as it gives 25 locomotives by name together with some details of types and cylinder dimensions. All but two of the locomotives listed in 1849 appear to have survived, but the fate of *Eagle* is not known, while *Runcorn*, almost certainly the locomotive of that name built by the Haigh Foundry in 1838, was withdrawn in 1854. A drawing still survives of various parts of a 'New engine — *Runcorn*', dated May 1852 and signed by Edward Borrows, but as there is no locomotive of that name in the 1855 list, the project may have been stillborn, or the locomotive built under another name.

A list of the St Helens Railway locomotive stock in 1855, laid out to correspond with the numerical order of the 1864 list in the next section, is given below. Comparison of the two will show that only six locomotives, *Navvie, John Smith, Swallow, Hero, Alma* and *Goliath* were still in existence under the same name at the LNWR takeover, but others such as *Resurgam* almost certainly survived under a different identity with or without rebuilding. In several cases, such as *Saracen, Scorpion* and *Mersey*, names were transferred directly to new acquisitions, as was also the custom on the LNWR.

### *St Helens Railway Locomotive Stock — January 1855*

| *Name* | *Type* | *Driving Wheels* | *Cylinders* | *Builder* | *Building Date* | *Date of Purchase* |
|---|---|---|---|---|---|---|
| | | ft in | in | | | |
| Navvie (Navvy) | 0-4-0 | (4 6) | ? | ? | ? | ? |
| St Helens | 0-4-0 | (5 0) | 13 × 18 | Haigh Foundry | 1838 | 10/38 |
| Widnes | 0-4-0 | 4 6 | 13 × 18 | Bury | 1834 | 5-6/34 |
| Director | 0-4-0 | ? | ? | ? | ? | |
| Swan | 0-4-0 | (4 6) | 13 × 20 | Jones, Turner & Evans | (1838) | (3/38) |
| John Smith | (0-4-0) | (4 0) | ? | (Bury) | ? | (1844) |
| Blackbrook | (0-4-0) | 4 6 | 14 × 22 | St H R | 1849 | — |
| Resurgam | 2-2-0T | 5 0 | 9 × 15 | Adams | 1850 | 5/50 |
| Swallow | 2-4-0 | 5 0 | (12 × 18) | L & M | 1841 | 3/50 |
| Sphinx | 0-4-2 | 5 0 | 14 × 18 | Melling | 1841 | 4/51 |
| Sutton | 0-4-2 | (5 0) | 12½× 18 | (Stephenson) | (1831) | 2/52 |
| Saracen | 0-4-2 | (5 0) | 14¾× 18 | Melling | 1842 | 2/52 |
| Garston | (2-4-0) | (5 0) | 14 × 22 | ? | ? | (1852) |
| Star | 2-2-2 | (5 0) | (12¼× 18) | L & M | 1844 | 2/52 |
| Scorpion | 0-4-2 | (5 0) | (14¼× 18) | Melling | 1842 | 2/52 |
| Mersey | (2-2-2) | (5 0) | 13 × 18 | (Tayleur) | (1838) | 4/51 |
| Britain | 2-4-0 | (5 0) | 13⅛× 20 | L & M | 1843 | 12/53 |
| Lapwing | 2-4-0 | (5 0) | 13 × 20 | L & M | 1843 | 9/53 |
| Queen | 2-2-2T | 5 0 | 10 × 16 | Fairbairn | 1851 | Before 4/53 |
| Sun | 2-2-2 | (5 0) | (12¼×18) | (L & M) | (1842) | (12/54) |
| Raven | (2-4-0) | (5 0) | 13 × 18 | (L & M) | (1843) | (12/54) |
| Rocket | 2-4-0 | 5 0 | 12³⁄₁₆× 18 | (L & M) | (1845) | (9/55) |
| Hero | 0-4-2 | 4 6 | 14⅜× 22 | St H R | 1853 | — |
| Alma | 2-4-0 | 5 0 | 12¼× 18 | ? | ? | ? |
| Goliath | 0-4-2 | 4 6 | 14⅜× 22 | St H R | 1854 | — |

*Notes*
1. Information which cannot be fully authenticated is shown in brackets.
2. Cylinder dimensions may differ from normally accepted sizes due to 'boring out' or 'linering up', but are in accordance with contemporary data.

It would appear that the locomotive *Swan* was sold to the Government for £1,303 for service in the Crimea, where a railway was being constructed to provide support services for the army. The LNWR Executive Committee minutes for 27 September 1855 record the sale of two old Northern Division engines to the St Helens Railway for £1,000, but no details are given. The minutes of the same committee for 9 May 1856 indicate that No 238 *Ribble* — as far as is known a Bury type 0-4-0 — was sold to the local company.

Meanwhile James Cross had not been idle in the company's own workshops. In 1855 he rebuilt the old 0-4-0 No 6 *John Smith*, and in the following year produced an 0-4-2, which became No 4 *Hercules*. Cross was authorised to sell *Mersey* for £300 in July 1857, while in the same year he rebuilt No 18 *Lapwing* from an older engine, and completed the extensive reconstruction of the ancient 0-4-0 No 1 *Navvie* (or *Navvy*), in which its driving wheels were reduced from 4ft 6in to 4ft 4in.

On 10 November 1858, Cross was authorised to purchase two locomotives from the Eastern Counties Railways for £800, but it is believed this transaction did not ultimately occur. Two Bury coal engines (former Manchester & Birmingham Railway Nos 28 and 29) were sold by the LNWR for £1,100 in December 1858, and in the same month the purchase of yet another second hand engine was noted in the minutes, but no details are given.

29 December 1858 was a red letter day for the company, as the secretary announced that two new 0-6-0 tender engines had been ordered from Sharp & Company. When delivered in the following April, these became Nos 30 *Severn* and 31 *Shannon*, but by April 1864 *Severn* was No 29 and *Shannon* No 22, while the former was renumbered 19 later in the same year.

By the middle of 1860 the St Helens Railway stock had risen to an all time high of 31 locomotives, together with 24 passenger coaches and 410 waggons. In April of the same year a Sharp Roberts 0-4-2 was purchased from the LNWR for £700 and became No 2 *Trent*. Cross was also working on a four coupled engine, possibly the 0-4-2 No 27 *Dee*, which may well have replaced an earlier engine of the same name.

Early in the same year, a scheme was formulated to allow traders to hire locomotives for their private use on a daily basis. A pilot scheme with six traders was introduced in August, and in the first month the income was £2,756 14s 7d against the estimate of £2,659, so the company decided to widen its scope. A detailed prospectus was issued on 15 December 1860.

In 1861, Cross began trials to evaluate the performance of the patent spring tyres, developed by William Bridges Adams, by this time engineer of the North London Railway. He fitted them to No 18 *Lapwing*, and proved their superiority over other more standard tyres fitted to *Hercules*, *Hero* and *Dee*. In due course he fitted spring tyres to *Clyde*, and to his most well known locomotive *Raven*. The reasons for carrying out adhesion trials on the St Helens Railway are given by Adams — 'This line is one of the most remarkable for its heavy gradients and sharp curves, the gradients being 1 in 35, 1 in 70 and 1 in 85, while the curves are of 300ft and 500ft radius, and moreover the points and crossings are very frequent, twelve miles of sidings occuring in a distance of two miles from the St Helens station.'

Apart from the half yearly reports giving rolling stock totals, there is no really concrete locomotive information until the 1864 working timetable, which together with the lists made at Crewe after the LNWR takeover, enable us to piece together details of the stock at that time, as well as the ultimate fate of most of them.

*Disposal of the Locomotive Stock*

28 locomotives passed into the hands of the LNWR, only No 19 *Queen* being sold to the Blackpool & Lytham Railway, almost certainly before the publication of the April 1864 timetable list in which it still appears. Only 21 locomotives valued at £20,850 remained in stock at the end of November 1864, as the LNWR did not take kindly to the motley collection it had acquired, and within a year of the takeover it had disposed of a further thirteen.

*St Helens Railway Locomotives handed over to LNWR August 1864*

| *No.* | *Name* | *Type* | *Driving Wheels* | *Cylinders* | *Builder* | *Building Date* |
|---|---|---|---|---|---|---|
| | | | ft in | in | | |
| 1. | Navvie | 0-4-0 | 4 4 | 11 × 18 | (Bury) | (1834) |
| 2. | Trent | 0-4-2 | 4 6 | 14 × 20 | Sharp Roberts | 1842 |
| 3. | Irwell | 0-6-0 | ? | ? | ? | ? |
| 4. | Hercules | 0-4-2T | 4 6 | 14½× 22 | St H R | 1856 |
| 5. | Swan | 2-2-2 | ? | ? | ? | ? |
| 6. | John Smith | 0-4-0 | 4 6 | 15 × 22 | (Bury) | (1844) |
| 7. | Eden | (0-4-2) | (4 6) | (14 × 22) | (St H R) | (1849) |
| 8. | Sankey | (2-2-0T) | (5 0) | (9 × 15) | (Adams) | (1850) |
| 9. | Swallow | 2-4-0 | 5 0 | (12 × 18) | Dewrance | 1841 |
| 10. | Ribble | 0-4-0 | (5 0) | (14 × 22) | Bury | (1847) |
| 11. | Tyne | 0-6-0 | 4 6 | 14½×22 | (Bury) | ? |
| 12. | Saracen | 0-6-0 | ? | ? | ? | ? |
| 13. | Forth | 0-4-2 | (4 9) | ? | ? | ? |
| 14. | Star | 0-4-2 | (5 0) | ? | ? | ? |
| 15. | Scorpion | 0-6-0 | ? | ? | ? | ? |
| 16. | Mersey | 0-6-0 | ? | ? | ? | ? |
| 17. | Britain | 0-6-0 | ? | ? | ? | ? |
| 18. | Lapwing | 0-6-0T | 4 0 | ? | St H R | ? |
| 19. | Severn | 0-6-0 | 4 8 | 16 × 22 | Sharp Stewart | 1859 |
| 20. | Sun | (2-2-2) | 5 0 | 12¼× 18 | L & M | 1842 |
| 21. | Raven | 2-4-2T | 5 1 | 15 × 20 | St H R | 1863 |
| 22. | Shannon | 0-6-0 | 4 8 | 16 × 22 | Sharp Stewart | 1859 |
| 23. | Hero | 0-4-2 | 4 6 | 14½× 22 | St H R | 1853 |
| 24. | Alma | 2-4-0 | 5 0 | 12 × 18 | St H R | ? |
| 25. | Goliath | 0-4-2 | 4 6 | 14⅜× 22 | St H R | 1854 |
| 26. | Clyde | 0-4-2 | 4 6 | 15 × 20 | St H R | 1863 |
| 27. | Dee | 0-4-2 | 4 6 | ? | St H R | 1860 |
| 28. | Lune | (0-4-0) | (4 0) | ? | (Bury) | (1846) |

*Notes*

1. Information which cannot be fully authenticated is shown in brackets.
2. Cylinder dimensions may differ from normally accepted sizes duc to 'boring out' or 'linering up', but are in accordance with contemporary information.
3. *Rebuilding Dates*
   The following locomotives are known to have been rebuilt by James Cross on the St Helens Railway:
   1 Navvie (1857), 6 John Smith (1855), 9 Swallow (1857), 18 Lapwing.
4. *Sharp's Works Numbers:*
   No 2, 199: No 19, 1129, No 22, 1130.

5. *LNWR Renumbering*
The St Helens Railway locomotives were renumbered by the LNWR in their original numerical order in the series 1367-1394. Only 7 survived to undergo any further renumbering:

| | | |
|---|---|---|
| 1372 (6 John Smith) | became | 1197 (9/65) |
| 1375 (9 Swallow) | " | 1200 (1/66) |
| 1382 (16 Mersey) | " | 1132 (10/65) |
| 1385 (19 Severn) | " | 1210 (12/67), 1817 (11/71) |
| 1387 (21 Raven) | " | 1226 (12/67), 1818 (11/71), 3040 (11/86) |
| 1388 (22 Shannon) | " | 1267 (12/67), 1819 (11/71) |
| 1390 (24 Alma) | " | 1125 (1/66), 1816 (11/71) |

6. *Reports to LNWR Locomotive Committee*
The sale of certain locomotives from the St Helens Railway was specifically recorded in reports to the LNWR Locomotive Committee:
19/1/65 — 1370 ( 4 Hercules), 1373 (7 Eden)
15/2/65 — 1384 (18 Lapwing), 1389 (23 Hero)
10/3/65 — 1395 (27 Dee)
12/4/65 — 1367 ( 1 Navvie)
19/5/65 — 1378 (12 Saracen)
14/7/65 — 1392 (26 Clyde)
15/9/65 — 1377 (11 Tyne)
14/1/70 — 1132 (16 Mersey)
8/12/71 — 1197 ( 6 John Smith)

Seven locomotives, No 3 *Irwell*, No 8 *Sankey*, No 10 *Ribble*, No 13 *Forth*, No 17 *Britain*, No 25 *Goliath* and No 28 *Lune*, were cut up more or less immediately for a variety of defects, which made repair uneconomic.

Four locomotives, No 2 *Trent*, No 5 *Swan*, No 14 *Star* and No 20 *Sun* were sold to the celebrated contractor, Isaac Watt Boulton. Three of these are then lost to view, but there is a long section dealing with *Trent* in the 'Chronicles of Boulton's Siding' by A R Bennett, including a photograph taken in 1866. *Trent* remained with Boulton for some years, undergoing a variety of adventures, and being rebuilt as a six coupled saddle tank in May 1871. After some further use Boulton sold it to the Chell Ironstone Mines in August 1873 for £850.

Four locomotives were sold in 1864 to James Cross, the former St Helens Railway engineer, who after his dismissal by the LNWR, had set up in business with his able assistant, Edward Borrows, in the old Locomotive Works at Sutton. There they built and rebuilt a variety of locomotives, including the first Fairlie 0-4-4-0 for the Neath & Brecon Railway. They also built a few four-coupled well tanks, whose design was then perpetuated by Borrows in his own locomotive works. Over fifty were built, the last under licence as late as 1929 by Kerr, Stuart & Company Ltd, and at least three have been preserved.

Cross purchased No 1 *Navvie*, No 4 *Hercules*, No 18 *Lapwing* and No 23 *Hero* for a total of £2,550. What happened to *Navvie* and *Lapwing* is not known, but *Hero* and *Hercules* both passed to the Bristol Port Railway & Pier Company as 0-4-2 tank engines. Although

*Hercules* started life as a tender engine, it was certainly rebuilt as a tank before the locomotive tyre trials of 1861. *Hero* was probably rebuilt by Cross prior to its sale to the BPR. Both remained with the BPR until the company was taken over by the GW & Midland Railways on 1 September 1890. Then No 1 *Hercules* went to Yorkshire, while No 2 *Hero* went to Abergorki Colliery near Mountain Ash. A photograph exists of the latter as *Duty* at Abergorki, and it is likely that it survived to become the locomotive *Severn* on the Shropshire & Montgomeryshire Railway, where it spent much of its working life on the Criggion branch before being broken up in April 1937.

Six other St Helens Railway locomotives were sold directly to individual contractors within a year of thc takeover. No 7 *Eden*, a four coupled tender engine, went to Mr W Hayes of Strangeways Hall Colliery at Wigan in January 1865 for £550. The 0-4-2 No 27 *Dee* was sold to Thomas Jackson of Eltham Park, Kent, for £1,500 in the following month. No 12 *Saracen* (an 0-6-0) went to James Livesey of London for £1,150 less £100 commission, which indicates that Livesey was an agent acting for a third party. Nothing is known of their subsequent career, but No 15 *Scorpion*, another 0-6-0, was sold in June 1865 to Mr Davis of Craven Arms for an unknown amount. It is reasonably certain that this became *Plowden* on the Bishops Castle Railway, which was opened on 24 October of the same year. It remained on the BCR for some nine years, including a period of running as a 2-4-0 with the leading coupling rods removed, but was broken up about 1874 without seeing use elsewhere.

The 0-4-2 tender engine No 26 *Clyde* was sold for £1,700 in July 1865 to Thomas Monk, a contractor at Seacombe near Birkenhead. It may very well have been used on the Hoylake Railway, which was under construction at that time. The last of the locomotives sold in 1865 was another 0-6-0, No 11 *Tyne*, which went to Benjamin Piercy for £1,250. It was renamed *Chancellor*, and worked the inaugural train on the Wrexham, Mold & Connah's Quay Railway on 1 January 1866, after being used on ballast trains during its construction. After repair in the Cambrian Railway works at Oswestry in 1867, it was scrapped between 1874 and 1876.

The remaining seven St Helens Railway locomotives did not remain long on their native ground. The 0-6-0 No 16 *Mersey* received a new boiler at Wolverton in September 1866, and was then sold to William Moss of Stafford for £450 in January 1870.

Three locomotives, No 6 *John Smith*, No 9 *Swallow*, No 24 *Alma*, all found their way to the Cromford & High Peak Railway. *Swallow* appears to have worked almost exclusively on the Cromford Junction section from its arrival in April 1865, until stopped for repairs in October 1869. Presumably it was then sent to Crewe, and was sold to Boulton in February 1871 for £150 'cash before delivery — less tubes'.

No 6 *John Smith* stayed on the High Peak from May 1865 to February 1870, working mainly on the section from Ladmanlow to Hurdlow and Hopton Top. Several contractors were interested in it, but sales fell through at the last minute, until it went to Barnes & Beckett of Nuneaton for £450 in December 1871.

The third locomotive, the 2-4-0 No 24 *Alma* had a much more complicated time. From its arrival on the High Peak in April 1865, it paid no less than five visits to Crewe, before its sale to Boulton for £400 in January 1874. At the end of 1873, its value had been assessed as £500, while the other three remaining St Helens Railway engines on the LNWR were assessed as follows: *Severn* (£2,100), *Shannon* (£2,150), *Raven* (£2,500).

*Alma* went off to the Whitland & Taf Vale Railway (later Whitland & Cardigan Railway) with Boulton himself on the footplate. It worked subsequently on the Lincoln & Barnetby Railway, and in due course was converted to a saddletank, being renamed *Rigg* after John Rigg of Crewe Works — one of Boulton's oldest friends. In December 1875, *Rigg* was hired to the Girvan & Portpatrick Junction Railway, together with two other of Boulton's locomotives. While at Girvan someone let the water out of the boiler one Saturday night, and when the driver lit up the following evening, he did not notice anything amiss until the firebox was ruined, and all the lagging burnt off the boiler. The crippled engine came back to Ashton in September 1876, and was then cut up in Ardwick yard.

Two of the remaining three St Helens Railway locomotives, *Severn* and *Shannon*, had relatively long but not well documented lives. Both were rebuilt in 1871, the latter possibly as an 0-6-0 tank engine. *Shannon* was withdrawn as No 1819 in March 1880, and *Severn* as No 1817 in January 1883.

The St Helens Railway locomotive, which lasted longest in LNW ownership, and probably the only one to be really well known, was the 2-4-2 tank No 21 *Raven*, generally called *White Raven*, as it was once painted in a striking white livery. Although possibly using some parts from the previous engine of that name, it was for all practical purposes a new engine designed and built by Cross at Sutton, and completed at the beginning of November 1863. Fitted with radial axleboxes on both leading and trailing axleboxes, so that the effective rigid axlebase was only 8 ft, *Raven* was designed as a passenger engine, but was ideal for tackling steep gradients with curves as sharp as 200 ft radius. It was tested in a variety of activities — it could haul a passenger train of 100 tons on the level over 60 mph, but experienced little difficulty on a wet day in hauling a 72 ton coal train up a gradient of 1 in 36 round a curve of 440 ft radius, or hauling 250 ton coal trains on gradients of 1 in 200. It was then sent off to the North London Railway for further trials, but Cross was always at pains to emphasise that it was not an experimental locomotive, but designed for everyday use.

In the 1870s it was rebuilt by the LNWR as a 2-4-0 tender engine, with 5 ft coupled wheels and 15 in × 22 in cylinders, but without the capacious cab it had in its early days. It ran for a time on services between Crewe, Shrewsbury and Stafford, but ended its day working special wool trains between Crewe and Huddersfield. It was withdrawn in July 1888 as No 3040, having survived its fourth renumbering in November 1886.

## CHAPTER VIII

# PASSENGER SERVICES

In the early years of the nineteenth century the inhabitants of St Helens could travel with relative ease to Bolton, Leeds and York by stage-coaches, which ran via Wigan or Newton. There was also a twice daily coach to Liverpool, passing through Prescot, where it made somewhat unsatisfactory connections with coaches to the south. In 1827, several local business men including Peter Greenall, purchased a small coach, which they called 'The Regulator' and hired it out to a contractor to take advantage of the growing traffic to and from Liverpool.

On the opening of the first section of the St Helens Railway, the company did not seem disposed to take advantage of the potential for passenger traffic along the L & M, so it was left to local residents to purchase a small horse drawn carriage, and run this along the railway between the town station near Peasley Cross Bridge and St Helens Junction. Agreement was reached in September 1832 that the promoters would pay the railway 25 per cent of the takings, while the contractor could also carry small items of freight on similar terms, and erect a small warehouse on company land at an annual rent of 4d per sq yd.

In March 1833, not long after the opening of the main line, Thomas Kidd, one of the directors, offered to operate a passenger coach over the line to Runcorn Gap at his own expense for a trial period of a fortnight. He suggested this should not be horse drawn, but attached to a locomotive. As no further references occur in the company minutes, the suggestion seemingly fell on stony ground. Nevertheless, in September 1833 the company hired two second-class coaches from the L & M at £1 a month each to run between the town and the junction and down to Runcorn Gap. These were scheduled to be attached to the rear of coal trains, but if only a few passengers wished to travel, they were generally accommodated in the engine tender.

Sir George Head in his book 'A Home Tour through the Manufacturing Districts of England in the Summer of 1835' found the horse drawn carriage still in operation on the line down to the junction at the time of his visit, and has this to say: '. . . we all got into one large covered vehicle, and were dragged at a foot pace, by a single horse, along the branch railroad, about a mile in length, that leads to the town . . . it must be confessed that the present mode of conveyance was as disagreeable and slow as can well be imagined.'

But some improvements to the services between town and junction had been made, because the St Helens Railway had both bought some coaches from the L & M, and also had arranged for through coaches from Manchester to be attached to at least one train a day for the benefit of passengers to and from Southport, for whom St Helens was a convenient railhead. In fact the L & M timetable for 1836 shows five trains on weekdays, all second-class, by which passengers from Manchester or Liverpool could reach St Helens. Only two trains made connection on Sundays, as was the case every day for travellers to Runcorn Gap, for as Sir George Head so beautifully put it: "It behoves not those people to whom time is of value, to travel by the branch railroad from St Helens to Runcorn; for as previously hinted, it by no means follows that because arrangements have been made to convey trains of coal waggons from one end of a line to the other, accidental passengers are to be equally favoured in their transit." The practice of attaching passenger coaches to the rear of freight trains wherever possible, was reconfirmed as the official policy on 10 August 1835, about the time of Head's visit. Space precludes the inclusion of the vivid and lengthy description of his three hour journey over the line to Runcorn Gap, with its delays and the hazardous descent of the inclined plane in a passenger coach pursued by a locomotive.

The "Appendix to the Second Report of the Select Committee on the State of Communications by Railways 1839" indicates that 26,290 passengers used the railway during 1838. But the first edition of 'Bradshaw's Railway Timetable', published on 19 October 1839, contains no official timetable for the railway, merely giving details of trains and fares in footnotes to the L & M and Bolton & Leigh Railways' timetables. By this time there were three connections into trains to Runcorn Gap, but rather surprisingly the fares were 6d cheaper than those to St Helens, although the former was about three times as far from the junction. Perhaps this was some consolation for the inconvenience of travelling to the local company's southern terminus, for, despite several purchases of rolling stock since Head's visit, things had hardly improved, as an irate traveller writing to the 'Manchester Courier' in 1840 amply demonstrates: "The writer of this paragraph booked himself by the quarter to six o'clock train from St Helens to Runcorn Gap and received a ticket from the book-keeper at the former place. At ten minutes to six the train — one coach — started, and in a few minutes arrived at the foot of the incline which carried the railway across the Liverpool to Manchester line. Here Runcorn pasengers alight, and a walk to the stationary engine followed. There the 'Parr' engine, with a train of coal waggons, was waiting. After some ten minutes' delay, the writer was told to mount the tender of the engine, his carriage being there to take him in the end of the journey. Another short ride brought him to the top of the second incline, on reaching which he was told to dismount from the coal box and walk on to Runcorn some two miles distance. After a walk and a wait he was picked up by the 'Runcorn' engine and that finally arrived at the station at Runcorn Gap at twenty five minutes past seven, having travelled the whole line of the Runcorn Gap & St Helens Railway some seven miles in the amazing short space of one hour and forty minutes, which is about five minutes longer than would take a tolerable pedestrian to walk over the same distance."

Details supplied to the Board of Trade in 1842 show that no third-class accommodation was provided, and that a passenger vehicle was still sometimes marshalled behind coal waggons, but the company had also persuaded the L & M to provide a first-class carriage on certain through trains to and from St Helens against a minimum guarantee of £100 per annum. A St Helens Railway timetable dated 14 October 1842, while showing services and connections to various towns in Lancashire, and even giving advice to intending passengers to Birmingham and London, makes no mention of trains to Runcorn Gap. This would seem to sum up the company's continuing attitude to passenger services over that section, which was still bedevilled by the operation of the inclined planes.

Official returns reviewing operations for the second half of 1845 indicate that 55,882½ passengers were booked at St Helens Railway stations. The company's timetables for the following year show no less than eleven trains in each direction between St Helens and the junction, of which eight were first and second class, and the remaining three Parliamentary. The Report of the Commissioners for Railways for 1847, which reviewed the provision of so-called 'cheap trains' to convey third class passengers, indicated that the local company offered these on ten trains a day. As the requirements, quite apart from suitable seats, protection from the weather and a fare of less than 1d per mile, included a speed of 12 mph, these certainly could not operate on the Runcorn Gap line. In the year ending 30 June 1847, the company carried 128,020 passengers, of which 73,499 were designated as 'Parliamentary', but only brought in £1,147 compared with £1,341 from the smaller number of higher class passengers.

The steep gradient out of Runcorn Gap led to painfully slow progress on the main line towards St Helens, despite the contention that the average speed of trains was 8 mph, and it is recorded that a young man named Thomas Whitby, by running at full speed, was able to catch up with the train he had just missed. So it is quite possible to believe the story that the station master at Runcorn Gap actually did issue latecomers with a ticket and say 'Now hurry yourselves — she's not long started, and if you look sharp, you'll catch her up.'

But the reconstruction and doubling of the line in the late forties, which eliminated the inclined planes, enabled the journey time for passenger trains to and from Runcorn Gap to be reduced to approximately 25 minutes, at which it remained until their withdrawal almost exactly a century later. A significant increase in passengers from 59,975 in the first half of 1849 to 91,941 in the same period of the following year clearly indicates the improvement in operation and services. Recognised intermediate stations at this time were at Appleton, Farnworth and Sutton, those at Clock Face and Peasley not making their appearance until some years later.

*The Last Twelve Years*

The opening of the Garston line on 1 July 1852 gave increased impetus to passenger traffic, particularly as on 2 August it was decided to permit through bookings to Liverpool, which included the journey by omnibus from the terminus of the railway to Castle Street in the city centre. Some problems were encountered in inclement weather, when first-class passengers found that their inside seats had been taken by third-class passengers, who paid a 2d supplement. But this was resolved in March of the following year, when the omnibus proprietor was instructed not to let any third-class passengers inside until all outside seats had been filled.

The timetable for May 1853 offered a weekday service of twelve trains a day between St Helens and Runcorn Gap, for the most part on a regular hourly interval, with trains leaving St Helens on the half hour and Runcorn Gap at five minutes to the hour. Alternate trains at two hourly intervals served Garston and the temporary station at Whitecross in Warrington. On Sundays there were four trains each way between St Helens and Runcorn Gap, with four to Garston and three to Warrington.

A ferry boat left Runcorn half an hour before the departure of the trains from Runcorn Gap and provided reasonably adequate connections, to ensure which the railway company in March 1850 had agreed to pay £3 a week in winter and £4 in summer, so that one boat could be reserved exclusively for railway passengers. Sir George Head, although he had not seen the ferry at its worst, made some scathing remarks about it, and even after the St Helens Railway had taken a 21 year lease for £920 per annum from 1 February 1854, there were times when even two boats could not cope. Irate passengers were often to be found at the water's edge . . . '. . . some denouncing the ferry proprietors, others more modestly expressing their determination if they could only meet with a Director, to treat him gratuitously to the blessings of infant Baptism'. Although the LNWR Runcorn Bridge, which incorporated a footpath, was soon to span the river, the ferry served vehicular traffic for a further forty years, until the well known transporter bridge was opened on 20 May 1905. This was closed on the opening of the new road bridge across the Mersey on 21 July 1961, and later dismantled.

As more connections were made with other railways, and the

resultant interchange traffic continued to increase, through passenger workings became of greater importance. On 14 September 1855 the company decided to run through carriages from St Helens to Warrington and Garston whenever practicable, and provide additional transfer facilities to and from the L & M main line. Excursion traffic also began to play an ever more important role in the life of the railway, as local residents headed for the seaside. In August 1856 Pilkingtons took 1,300 people to Southport by train, albeit by a somewhat circuitous route, and after the opening of the Rainford line in 1858, both private and works outings to the seaside were to achieve a popularity which only waned during the middle years of the present century.

Throughout the mid fifties it is possible to keep a monthly check on the St Helens Railway passenger services from the attractively headed timetables in the local press. But our most detailed knowledge of St Helens Railway operation comes from the working timetable, which came into force on 1 April 1864. This covers all regularly scheduled passenger and freight workings between Rainford Junction and Runcorn Gap, together with trips serving the various colliery and industrial branches, although as the Warrington-Garston line was by then leased to the LNWR it does not figure in the timetable. Passenger trains are printed in red and freights in black, with the name of the guard given at the top of the timing column. The most significant feature as far as passenger services are concerned is the continuing reduction in the number of trains between St Helens and Runcorn Gap, compared with those operating previously. On weekdays there were only five compared with the twelve running after the opening of the Garston line. On the other hand, there were no less than sixteen connections with LNW trains at St Helens Junction, and five workings in each direction on the Rainford line. No freight trains ran on Sunday, but there were three passenger trains to and from Rainford Junction and Runcorn Gap, with five running down to connect with the LNWR.

After the opening of the Edge Hill-Garston line on 15 February 1864, there were twelve trains in each direction between Warrington and Liverpool, and thus the St Helens directors' dreams of operating through trains to Liverpool were finally realised, albeit for only six months and on a line leased to the LNWR.

Passenger traffic originating on the St Helens Railway itself had built up from a reasonably static 20,000-30,000 passengers a year in the late thirties and forties to 135,420 in 1849, almost doubling in only two years to 266,013 in 1851. 1853 saw a further jump to 564,993, with a steady increase to 726,414 in 1858 after the opening of the Rainford line. Statistics, even from official sources, are not always consistent, and are found in the most unlikely places, such as those up to 1853, which come from the 'Ranger Report to the President of the General Board of Health on Sewerage, Drainage and the Supply of Water' dated 15 October 1855.

## CHAPTER IX

# THE LNWR TAKES OVER

The St Helens Railway Ditton-Garston line gained added significance as part of a new main line from Merseyside to the south, after the construction of the line from Acton Bridge. Seventeen million bricks were supplied by John Hutchinson for the construction of the bridge across the Mersey at Runcorn, which was formally opened on 21 May 1868. The bridge was taken into use a month later for local traffic into Runcorn, but the Acton Bridge line was not opened for freight until 1 February of the following year, with passenger services commencing from 1 April 1869.

Meanwhile the LNWR had promised expenditure of £100,000 for improvements to the track and stations it had taken over from the local company, including a bridge over the railway in St Helens and specific improvements at Sutton Oak, which had to be carried out within twelve months in accordance with the provisions of the 1864 Act. One of the major improvements was made to the layout at Runcorn Gap (or Widnes as the station was renamed on 1 September 1864), by building a deviation line to take most through traffic away from the level crossing over Waterloo Road, as well as from the flat crossing of the St Helens-Widnes and Warrington-Garston lines. This was to be achieved by building a loop line 1 mile, 2 furlongs 3 chains in length, leaving the existing Warrington-Widnes line near Carter House Bridge and curving northwards on an embankment to bridge the St Helens line, before descending to rejoin the Garston line near Marsh Road. A new station was to be provided on it to the west of the bridge over the St Helens line, to which it would be connected by a spur. A three-road engine shed was later built between the deviation and the connecting line to stable the locomotives employed in the area. Although in 1873 it was approved to hold six locomotives, only six years later 26 were allocated there, so constant improvements in accommodation were necessary.

The construction of the deviation was authorised by the LNWR (New Works & Additional Powers) England and Scotland Act of 5 July 1865. Several attempts were made to alter or extend its course, but none found favour, and it was eventually opened for freight traffic on 1 November 1869. The old station on the existing Warrington-Garston line was closed on 1 March of the following year to coincide with the opening of the new line and station to passenger traffic. A new station was opened at Ditton, between Widnes and Halewood on 1 May 1871, replacing the original station some 250 yards to the east.

The 1865 Act also authorised the construction of a branch some five miles in length from Huyton to St Helens, a revival of the GJ scheme of some twenty years earlier. This was to enter St Helens on a long viaduct, which crossed the Ravenhead branch and many of the internal glassworks' sidings, as well as cutting across the lines to the old station at Salisbury Street in order to reach the through station built in 1858. A branch just over half a mile in length from Peasley Cross on the original St Helens Railway line to the Broad Oak line to facilitate through running between St Helens and the Broad Oak and Blackbrook branches was also authorised.

But the inhabitants of Warrington were not at all happy with the LNWR, for having constructed a new station at Bank Quay to serve both the west coast main line and the former St Helens line which passed under it, Arpley station was closed on 16 November 1868, reputedly at only two days' notice. It was said that some 8,000 passengers used Arpley each week, as it was better sited for the town centre. The 'Warrington Guardian' was particularly scathing about the new Garston line facilities which it described as merely 'a covered shed, open in front, for all classes to herd in . . .' The resultant outcry forced the LNWR to make some concessions in the following year by agreeing to stop a couple of trains at Wilderspool Ticket Platform. No further progress was made until May 1871, when the implications of Section 29 of the Act authorising the construction of the Warrington & Altrincham Junction Railway were fully explored. This specified a station within 150 yeard of the level crossing on Wilderspool causeway, and the LNWR were forced to reopen Arpley station. They did this with somewhat ill grace on 2 October 1871, after completely refurbishing the building. To cater for local services, a small locomotive shed was also opened at Arpley in the 1880s.

Meanwhile developments were taking place in St Helens to provide new rail links with Liverpool and Wigan. Colliery owners in the latter area were very keen to gain access to the docks at Widnes and Garston, so that they could load and export their coal at cheaper rates than those in force at the port of Liverpool. The incorporation of the Lancashire Union Railways on 25 July 1864, which was strongly supported by the LNWR, gave sanction for the construction of various lines in the Wigan area, as well as a line from Haigh near Wigan, to St Helens, where it would join the St Helens Railway by a triangular junction just south of Peasley Cross. Although on 26 May of the following year the lines around Wigan were vested jointly in the Lancashire & Yorkshire and Lancashire Union Railways, the Wigan-St Helens line remained exclusively LU property. Alterations were made to its course both at the St Helens end, so it joined the Rainford branch at Gerard's Bridge, fifty chains north of St Helens station, and at the Wigan end, where it was to connect with the L & Y Liverpool-Wigan line at Pemberton. On

16 July 1866 the LUR was authorised to build two further lines in the St Helens area, the first 3 miles 12.5 chains in length from Garswood to the Blackbrook branch near Fleet Lane, with a second branch 60 chains in length to serve the newly opened Havannah Colliery, but in due course both were abandoned in their original form.

Despite some problems with the contractors, construction of the Wigan-Gerard's Bridge line started in earnest at the end of 1866, and the line was inspected for the Board of Trade by Colonel Hutchinson on 21 August 1869. He was not wholly satisfied with what he saw, and freight trains were not allowed to run into St Helens until 1 November. It had been intended to open the line for passengers on 15 November, but further inspections were required before this traffic could begin. It was passed for passenger train operation on 25 November, and services began on 1 December 1869, with trains stopping at the two intermediate stations of Garswood and Bryn. By virtue of the working agreements made in 1865 and 1866 the LNWR operated all passenger trains into St Helens, although the LYR still exercised its running powers to operate coal trains.

The line from Peasley Junction, just south of Ravenhead Junction on the Widnes line, to Pocket Nook Junction near Gerard's Bridge, was also improved, so that it could be used as an avoiding line to relieve growing congestion through the station, and it was taken into use in this form on 1 November 1869.

Meanwhile in 1868 work started on the construction of the line from Huyton to St Helens, but progress was slow, particularly through the sandstone cuttings near Thatto Heath. Nevertheless its impending but delayed opening, and the increasing traffic from the Wigan line caused the LNWR to build a new station at Shaw Street, St Helens. This was opened on 17 July 1871 for freight and passenger traffic after being in partial use for some weeks. The 1858 station, variously described as "a wretched little hole" and a "standing disgrace to the town", was closed on the same day, but its replacement, although it was to serve the town for 90 years, was not greeted with universal enthusiasm. The goods station was not connected from the south, but the junction was found at Pocket Nook, and all trains had to proceed there to be shunted onto the goods lines. The passenger station was described as a "fourth class" station, rather than the first class facility which the inhabitants had been led to expect. But although plans for additions and improvements were drawn up at various times, notably in 1877, 1883 and 1903, the main structure remained substantially the same throughout its life. After a series of delays, freight traffic commenced on the Huyton line on 18 December 1871, to be followed by passenger services on 1 January 1872. Intermediate stations were provided at Prescot and Thatto Heath, and a further station was opened at Eccleston Park in July 1891.

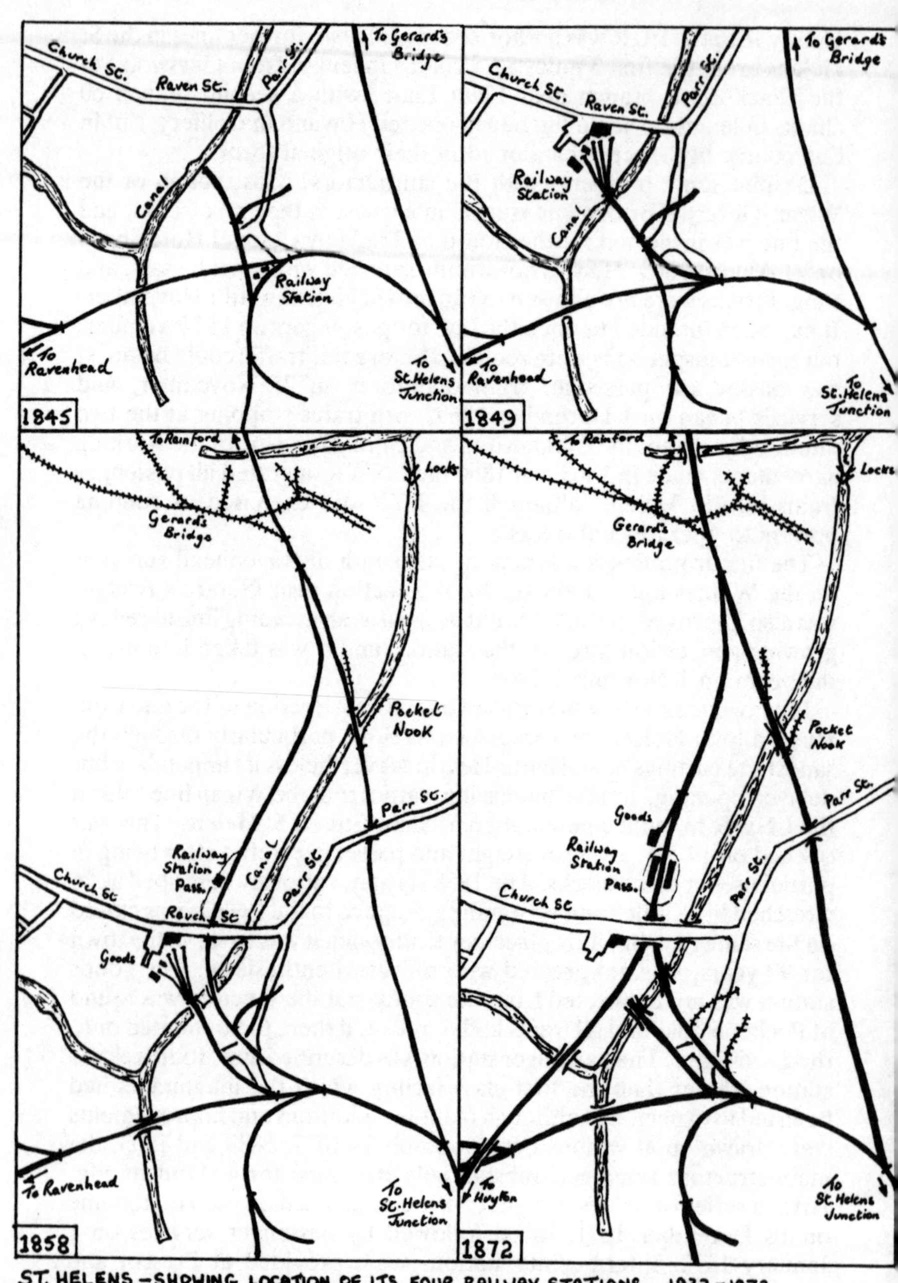


ST. HELENS – SHOWING LOCATION OF ITS FOUR RAILWAY STATIONS 1832–1872.

MAIN LINES (INCLUDING FREIGHT ONLY) MINOR INDUSTRIAL LINES

Although the LUR scheme to build an avoiding line for St Helens by providing a link from Garswood to the Blackbrook branch had been finally abandoned on 25 May 1871, the LNWR Act of 22 July 1878 authorised a much shorter link of 60 chains from the Blackbrook branch to a junction with the LU line at Carr Mill, to fulfil very much the same purpose. The contract for its construction was let to George Nowell for £4,300 on 18 June 1879, and the line was opened on 23 February 1880. The vesting of the LUR in the LNWR was authorised on 16 July 1883 by the LNWR (New Railways) Act, and completed that company's monopoly of the St Helens area.

Plans for improving operations at St Helens Junction were deposited for the 1881 Parliamentary session. The Widnes line was to be widened from a point near the connection to the former St Helens Railway Works, northwards to Sutton Oak Junction, a total distance of just over five furlongs. More important, however, were the proposals for a new double track line, just over four furlongs long, which on leaving the junction station, burrowed under the St Helens line and then climbed up to rejoin it on the west side at Sutton Oak Junction. These improvements were successfully carried out, and on 19 July 1887 the LNWR was authorised to widen some 5½ miles of the former LU line between Carr Mill Junction and Ince Moss Junction. The contract was let to Charles Braddock for £47,255 on 19 June 1889, and the additional two tracks taken into use on 16 October 1892. Two years later work began on a station at Carr Mill, and this first appeared in 'Bradshaw' in January 1896, but after a relatively short existence it was closed to all traffic from 1 January 1917.

*Dock and Canal Activities*

The new lines opened by the LNWR and those of the CLC, with which we will deal later, brought added importance to Garston Dock, and a direct curve from Allerton to Garston, to facilitate through running to and from Liverpool, was opened on 1 January 1873. This was closely followed in June 1875 by the opening of a new North Dock at Garston, while on 22 July 1878 the LNWR was authorised to widen almost six miles of line between Speke and Widnes, including the provision of additional lines running to the south of the Runcorn line east of Ditton, and then burrowing under it to gain access to Widnes. The two additional lines between West Deviation Junction in Widnes and Ditton Junction were opened on 2 February 1885, the quadrupling of the line between Ditton Junction and Speke Junction having been completed in the previous year.

On 1 March 1881 an additional passenger station was opened at Church Road, Garston, the original station then being renamed Garston Dock. A proposal for a further new dock at Garston was submitted as early as 1888, in the position and shape of the later

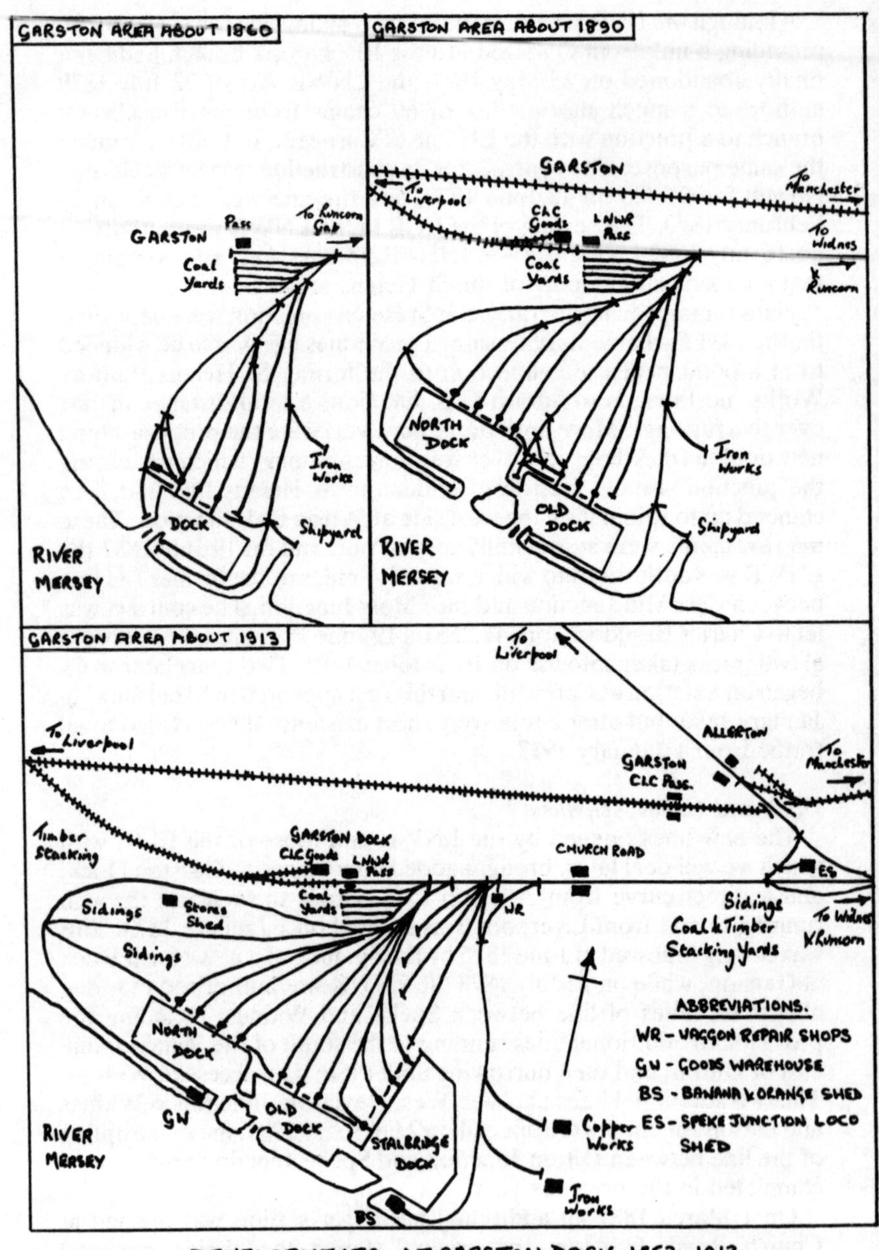


DEVELOPMENTS AT GARSTON DOCK 1853–1913.

———— ST HELENS RAILWAY & LNWR ++++++++ CHESHIRE LINES COMMITTEE.

NOT TO SCALE — SCHEMATIC LAYOUT IN DOCKS TO SHOW APPROX. LOCATION OF MAJOR ITEMS.

Stalbridge Dock, although this was not opened until February 1909, by which time over two million tons of coal alone were passing through the port. A sleeper depot was also established at Garston, although in due course this was transferred to its current site at Ditton Junction.

As mentioned earlier, when the LNWR was negotiating to take over the St Helens Railway, the local chemical manufacturers had made representations to get the canal tolls reduced from the maximum of 1s 0d to the pre-1848 level of 8d per ton. They were not wholly successful in this, but a reduction to 8d for coal and to 10d for other merchandise was indeed forthcoming. The traditional exemptions for limestone, soapers' waste, manure and materials for repairing roads, quays or wharves connected with the canal, or for the use of landowners, were continued in the 1864 Act, while dock dues and transfer charges for vessels were also reduced. All these provisions were again perpetuated in a further Act of 1891. Indeed the LNWR, far from continuing the powers of the 1845 Act to close those parts of the waterway which were not profitable, had given an undertaking to keep it all open, clean and in good repair. But by the 1870s chemical pollution had become so bad that the mortar of the retaining walls was seriously affected and crumbled dangerously at certain points. All this was costly to rectify, but as over half a million tons of merchandise still passed along the waterway each year, the LNWR was well satisfied with this acquisition.

## CHAPTER X

# THE INTRUDERS

Revised plans for the Garston & Liverpool Railway, supported by the MS & L and GN Railways, were deposited in November 1860, and proposed a line just over 4½ miles in length, starting from an end-on junction with the St Helens Railway at Dock Road, Garston, with a terminus in Liverpool at Parliament Street. Although the G & L line was sanctioned on 17 May 1861, a further Act in the following year authorised it to be cut back by about half a mile at the Liverpool end because of increases in cost, and its new terminus was at Brunswick Dock on the outskirts of the city. Running powers were granted over the St Helens and W & S Railways, and the line was opened on 1 June 1864, with omnibuses providing a connection between Brunswick and the railway offices at James Street in the city centre. A further 10 years were to elapse before the opening of the Liverpool Central Station & Railway on 1 March 1874 gave rail access to the centre of Liverpool.

After the demise of the St Helens Railway, the MS & L and GN Railways had to rely on the maintenance of their running powers over some 25 miles of track inherited by a far from friendly LNWR. Sir Edward Watkin attempted to overcome this problem with some haste, and his efforts bore fruit in the MS & L (Extension to Liverpool) Act of 6 July 1865. This authorised a totally new railway between Manchester and Garston, running from Old Trafford on the MSJA to a junction with the G & L near Cressington. A second line was to run from Glazebrook on this projected railway to Skelton Junction near Timperely on the Stockport, Timperley & Altrincham Junction Railway, which was then in the course of construction. On 16 July 1866, the Manchester-Garston line was vested in the Cheshire Lines Committee, which already incorporated the G & L, the Liverpool Central Station & Railway and the ST & AJ, together with three other short lines. Control had been vested in the MS & L and GN Railways by the Cheshire Lines Transfer Act of 5 July 1865, with the Midland Railway beginning its participation on 18 July 1866.

Meanwhile the MS & L had obtained powers to vary the route of the new line at the Manchester end, and also to provide a loop line through the centre of Warrington because of the public outcry elicited by the original scheme, which by-passed the town.

The trade depression of the late sixties delayed the completion of the new main line, and indeed it might never have been built if the Midland & GN Railways had accepted a proposal made by the LNWR in 1868. This proposed that the Garston-Warrington-Altrincham line now owned by the LNWR, and the CLC Altrincham-Stockport line, should become the joint property of the four companies involved, with the LNWR having a 50 per cent share, and the remaining 50 per cent shared between the CLC partners, who would enjoy access to Lime Street station in Liverpool. Nothing came of this, however, and work was resumed on the new line in the following year, which together with the loop line through Warrington, was opened from Skelton West Junction to Cressington Junction near Garston to freight on 1 March 1873. Passenger services started on 1 August, and the rest of the main line from Cornbrook Junction in Manchester to Glazebrook was opened to all traffic on 2 September of the same year. In May 1874, after the opening of the line to Liverpool Central, the CLC inaugurated a new express service between Manchester and Liverpool, and its services over the LNW lines via Garston and Broadheath were discontinued.

While Warrington was to be well served by the new CLC line, the nearest station to Widnes was at Farnworth, some 1½ miles from the town centre. Although it passed under the St Helens Railway north of the latter's Farnworth station, there was no physical connection to the local line. By the early seventies, Widnes had grown into an important industrial centre with over twenty sizeable chemical works, two copper works, two iron works and one soap factory. Two of these employed some 500 people, and a further five over 100. An efficient transport system was obviously needed, but although the LNWR had already opened its deviation line through the town, and by 1870 could boast of connections to no less than 47 factories in the area, it had tended to be rather autocratic in its dealings with industrialists, forcing them wherever possible to make connection with the original St Helens Railway line, rather than with the Garston-Warrington line, which gave more direct access to Liverpool and Manchester.

A proliferation of schemes for short inter-connected lines with frequently changing layouts, and often conflicting aims, characterised the period leading up to the construction of the Widnes loop line. Foremost among the industrialists, who were vociferous in their condemnation of the LNWR and its attitude, was John Bibby, a man involved in the business life of both St Helens and Liverpool. For many years he had been buying up poor quality land in Widnes between the St Helens and Warrington lines, with a view to founding a similar industrial estate to that being developed by John Hutchinson. By 1866 he owned 210 acres, and the impending construction of the LNW deviation line appeared an ideal opportunity for him, particularly if he could get the course altered to run over his land. Although the LNW proposals of 1867 for extending the deviation line would have done this very nicely, they were withdrawn after passing through the Commons. His displeasure at that decision was further increased, when an arbitrator reduced from £16,000 to £8,000 the price of two acres of land he had to sell to the LNWR for the deviation line. Moreover, when Bibby made a further request for rail connection to his land, he was offered only sidings from the north-south line. This unfortunately meant that he had to cross two yards of land owned by the Hutchinson Trustees, a privilege which would cost him dear, but he knew that no manufacturer would set up premises on his land without the benefit of rail connection. Bibby found an ally in Sir Richard Brooke, a neighbouring landowner, and together they investigated the possibilities of a branch across their land which, if provided with a triangular junction on the CLC line, would give direct connection to both Liverpool and Manchester.

Plans for the Widnes Railways were deposited in October 1871. These consisted of three interconnected lines, the first 1 mile 3 furlongs in length running due south from a westbound junction between Farnworth and Sankey stations on the CLC main line. The second line, which was just over a mile in length, made a junction with the first just before its termination, and ran due west to a terminus at Tanhouse Lane. The third line, only five furlongs in length, headed off north eastwards from this point to terminate in the Green Oaks area. Opposition from the LNWR was very fierce, and the proposals were withdrawn for resubmission in 1873, with a slight shortening of the third branch as the only modification. Long and acrimonious disputes took place before the Select Committee of the House of Commons, with the MS & L, in support of the local line, stating that it had no wish to take trade away from the LNWR, but merely to provide rail connections for the newer factories lying to the east and north of the existing lines, even though at that time no specific plans for any factories in that area had yet been made. Watkin himself lent weight to the case for a new line by pledging the MS & L to provide £40,000 to the cost of the project, and stated that even if the company would not support the project, he and certain friends would personally raise £60,000, if authority was given for the CLC or MS & L to use or work the line. In the evidence it was stated that annual railborne tonnage involved in the industrial life of Widnes amounted to 1,177,240 tons, of which over 100,000 tons were carried over the rapidly expanding lines of the Hutchinson Estate & Dock company. Despite the objections of the LNWR, which did not formally give up the struggle until June 1873, and the obvious weaknesses of the landowners' arguments, the Widnes Railway (Certificate & Railways Provisional Certificate Confirmation) Act of 7 July 1873 gave authority to build a three mile branch running from a point east of Ann Street in Widnes to a junction with the CLC line at Barrows Green, the original concept of three separate lines having been somewhat simplified. Capital of £60,000 was authorised, and the MS & L was empowered to subscribe up to two thirds of the required amount.

The independent existence of the Widnes Railway came to an end after only one year, well before it was opened to traffic, when it was transferred to the MS & L by the latter's Additional Powers Act of 16 July 1874. It would have been logical for the local line to be included in the CLC, but the GN objected to this, and so by the Act of 29 June 1875 it was vested in the Sheffield & Midland Railway Companies Committee, which later became the Great Central & Midland Joint Committee.

Meanwhile proposals for the Widnes (West) Junction Railway had also been submitted for the 1873 session. This line, which was just over two miles in length, was to run southwards to Moor Lane from a triangular junction with the CLC west of Farnworth, crossing over the Garston-Widnes line and under the LNWR Runcorn line before continuing westwards towards Ditton Iron Works. It was withdrawn during the 1873 session, mainly because of the lack of success attending a further proposal to link the CLC line with the St Helens line near Farnworth, which had naturally excited the vigorous opposition of the LNWR.

In October 1874 plans were submitted to the MS & L directors for an extension of the Widnes Railway to join the line once more being promoted by local landowners, which would in effect give a loop from the CLC passing through the centre of the town. This would start near the projected Widnes Railway passenger terminus at Tanhouse Lane, and, after being carried through the town on a 440 yard viaduct, effect a junction with the landowners' line. Provision was also made for a dock and an eastbound connection to the CLC line at Widnes Junction. Construction of these commenced at about the time the original Widnes Railway line was opened for freight traffic on 3 April 1877. The south to east curve to the CLC was pronounced complete on 20 March 1878, and received Board of Trade approval for goods traffic on 17 April. The westbound connection at Widnes Junction was removed on 29 February 1880, even though its remnants were used for waggon storage until the 1960s.

Well over 700 men were at work on the two projects, which were built by Logan & Hemingway and James Cross respectively. They involved some very heavy engineering works through the centre of the town, and on the line to Widnes Marsh, where connection was made to the Hutchinson Estate & Dock Railway. By the end of 1878 both were substantially complete, and freight services began on 1 July 1879. On 16 July the Board of Trade authorised the operation of passenger traffic on all the lines making up the Widnes loop, and these began on the opening of the new Central Station on 1 August 1879. To complete main line railway developments in Widnes a new station at Tanhouse Lane was opened on 1 September 1890.

*The MS & LR in St Helens*

In St Helens, too, there was a growing dissatisfaction with the LNWR's monopoly of the district and its rapidly expanding industry. By the early 1880s the town had some 60,000 inhabitants, and all its major industries — glass, coal, alkali and copper smelting — were still flourishing, together with a host of foundries and engineering establishments. One of the most important developments to affect the ultimate well-being of St Helens, and indeed the survival of part of the Rainford branch even today, was the decision by Pilkington Brothers to embark on the manufacture of cast plate glass in a new factory at Cowley Hill, which went into production in July 1876. Although other plate glass manufacturers collapsed in the trade depression towards the end of the century, Pilkingtons survived and flourished because of the technical advances it made in window glass production. Its ever increasing trade generated an immense volume of traffic for the railway, with a works complex served by its own extensive internal rail system. Copper smelting, which in 1889 still employed over 2,000 in six large factories in St Helens, soon went into decline as more copper ore was smelted close to the mines, and by the turn of the century all the large works had closed. The alkali works, too, with their antiquated Leblanc process of soda production, lost business in the face of foreign competition, and the introduction of more modern processes in the Cheshire factories of the United Alkali Company Ltd. At its formation in 1890 the company controlled 48 factories in the British Isles, including nine major works in St Helens and fourteen in Widnes.

But in the 1870s, when the major industries of the town were still flourishing, and coal mining in particular was linked in the minds of men with the need for better rail communications, the opening of the greater part of the Wigan Junction Railways to freight traffic in October 1879, even more than the new lines at Warrington and Widnes, once again aroused local feeling against the LNWR. Moreover, the opening of the Southport & Cheshire Lines Extension Railway of the CLC from Aintree to Southport on 1 September 1884, made industrialists in St Helens see the possibility of making their town the focal point of a line from Wigan to Southport and Liverpool. Plans were drawn up for an eighteen mile line from Lowton St Marys on the Wigan Junction Railways, running via Golborne and Ashton-in-Makerfield to St Helens, and thence via Dentons Green, Knowsley and Croxteth Park to a junction with the CLC at Fazakerley, from which point there would be easy access to both Southport and to the docks at Liverpool. But, when the St Helens & Wigan Junction Railway was sanctioned on 22 July 1885 to construct the full length of the line from Lowton St Marys to Fazakerley, only £210,000 in capital and £70,000 in loans was authorised, although it was envisaged that

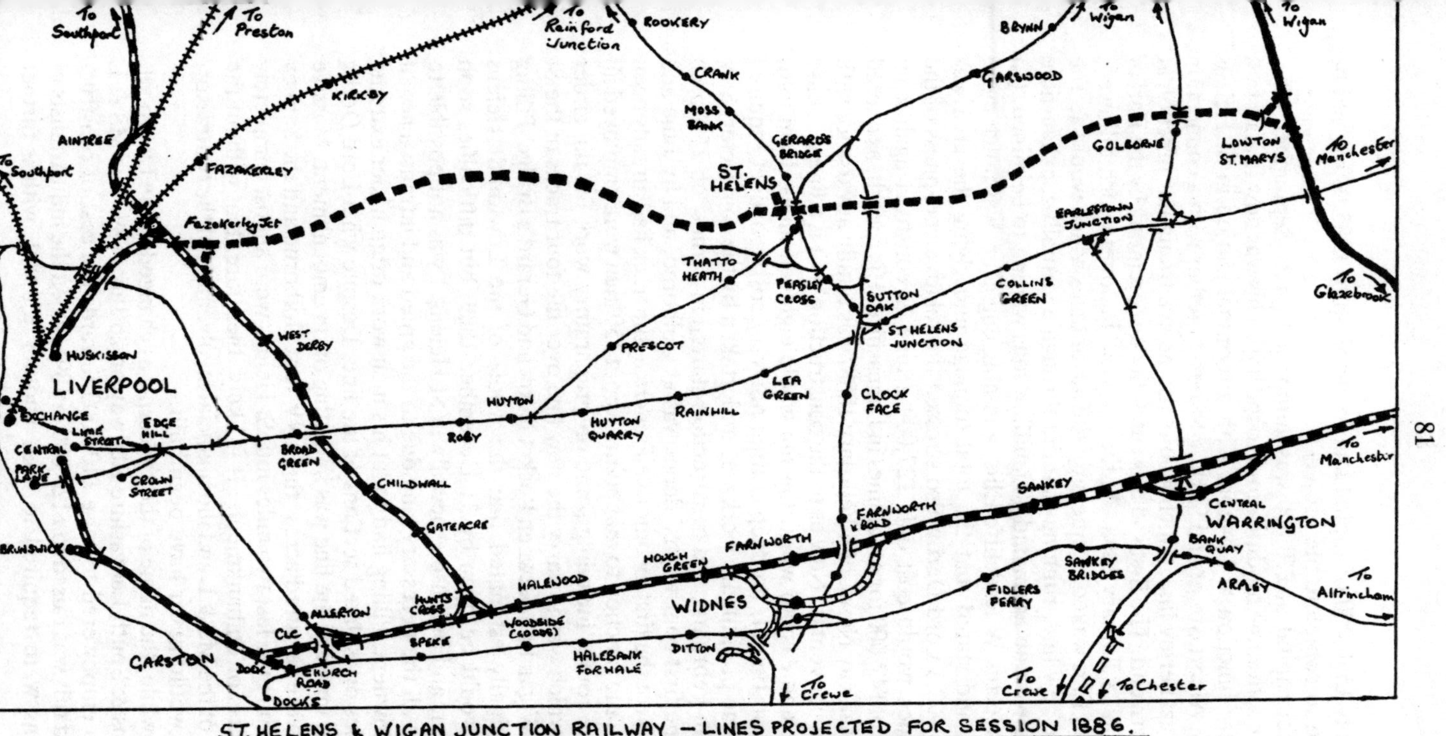


ST. HELENS & WIGAN JUNCTION RAILWAY — LINES PROJECTED FOR SESSION 1886.

INCORPORATING AMENDMENTS AND ADDITIONS TO THOSE AUTHORISED IN 1885.

ST. HELENS & WIGAN JUNCTION RAILWAY
MANCHESTER, SHEFFIELD & LINCOLNSHIRE RAILWAY
CHESHIRE LINES COMMITTEE
SHEFFIELD & MIDLAND COMMITTEE
LONDON & NORTH WESTERN RAILWAY.
LANCASHIRE & YORKSHIRE RAILWAY
BIRKENHEAD RAILWAY (GW & LNW JT.).

LAYOUT IN LIVERPOOL AREA VERY MUCH SIMPLIFIED — ONLY CERTAIN LINES & STATIONS SHOWN.

ultimately £550,000 of capital and loans of up to £183,000 would be required to complete the project.

Further capital of £70,000 was authorised on 25 September 1886, together with some modifications to the line. This was now to start by a triangular junction at Lowton, with a terminal station in St Helens between Albert Street and Stirling Street, together with a connection to the Fazakerley line, which would also have a triangular junction at its western end. The first sod was cut with due ceremony by the Earl of Derby on 28 January 1888. At the splendid banquet which followed, the noble Earl waxed eloquent on the advantages which would accrue from the new line, running as it did through a virtually inexhaustible coalfield with an estimated 400 million tons waiting to be mined. (In the prospectus W Radcliffe Ellis, a mining engineer, was much more precise, and stated that the total tonnage underlying the area was 423,706,902.) Lord Derby also stressed the relative cheapness of the line, which would cost only £27,000 a mile to construct against an average of £47,000 for other lines in Lancashire. His speech, as quoted in the 'Railway News' of 4 February 1888, was totally at variance with subsequent events: "Now as to the construction — it is a line . . . easy to make and easy to work. On the whole eighteen miles, I am told, there is no tunnel, no deep cutting nor very costly viaduct required . . ." Some preliminary work was undertaken by the contractor, S W Pilling, in February, and construction started in earnest on 21 March 1888. The first contractors' depot was at Golborne, and by June and the arrival of the first locomotive *Frederica*, the track had already been laid from the junction to that point. About 150 men were employed all along the route, including some on preparatory work for the girder bridge, which was to carry the new line over the four tracks of the St Helens-Wigan line between Pocket Nook and Gerard's Bridge. Pilling had originally estimated that the whole of the Lowton-St Helens section would be open by 31 December 1889, but difficulties soon beset him, and because especially in St Helens it was not possible to purchase all the necessary land due to the greed and intransigence of the landowners, Pilling had to let his men work often under extreme difficulties on isolated sections of the line. Despite what Lord Derby had said, much of the line was in cutting or on embankment. Massive bridges were required across the LNWR at Golborne and the Sankey Canal, while the last two miles into St Helens were almost completely on viaducts or embankments. It is likely, therefore, that without the backing of the MS & L and the financial involvement of the contractor, the line would never have been built.

Meanwhile, the name of the concern was changed to the Liverpool, St Helens & South Lancashire Railway on 26 July 1889. The MS & L was also empowered to raise £100,000 towards the cost of construction, and this was raised to £120,000 in 1891, when the industrialists of St Helens were required to raise another £50,000, with a further

£70,000 to be obtained by loans. All this and more was necessary to keep the company solvent until Pilling's perseverence paid off, and the 8¼ mile line between Lowton and St Helens was opened to freight traffic on 1 July 1895, almost ten years after its authorisation. The line, which was double from the junction to Ashton-in-Makerfield, and single thence to St Helens, was at first worked by the MS & L only as far as Golborne, trains being taken on to St Helens by contractors' locomotives, until through running by the MS & L began on 21 October 1895. It was confidently expected that passenger services would begin by the end of the year, but a further four years were to elapse before this took place.

Sanction was gained in 1897 for a second debenture issue of £150,000 to facilitate the doubling of the Ashton-St Helens section, and the raising of the whole line to passenger standards. The Act also authorised construction of a branch to Pilkingtons' Works at Cowley Hill, which was already served by the former St Helens Railway Rainford branch. The proposed Southport extension was abandoned on 21 July 1897, because of the general financial troubles of the company, and the unwillingness of St Helens industrialists to get involved in actively supporting the new line. This situation was to continue for the next four years, and work on the doubling of the existing line was frequently stopped, when the contractor became tired of receiving promises instead of money as payment for his efforts. In due course the line between Lowton Junction and Haydock Park was inspected and passed by Colonel Addison, so that passenger trains could be run for the race meeting on 10 February 1899. Pilling increased his forces on the line to 200 men, 5 boys, 14 horses and 3 locomotives, and managed to complete the second line of rails from Ashton-in-Makerfield to the eastern end of the bridge in St Helens by the beginning of June, but its completion was delayed by the late delivery of steelwork for the bridge. It was not until 19 December 1899 that the whole line was inspected by Lt-Col Von Donop, and pronounced fit for passenger traffic.

There was a formal opening ceremony on 2 January 1900 for directors and their guests, and public passenger services began on the following day. Five of the six trains in each direction on weekdays provided a through service to Manchester, although only one of the three Sunday trains afforded this facility. Intermediate stations were provided at Golborne, Ashton-in-Makerfield and Haydock, together with the special racecourse platforms at Haydock Park. Although the total area of the station and goods facilities at St Helens covered eight acres, only a single platform was provided, and at the opening the running line was still single from the station to the viaduct at Pocket Nook. In due course, as both the GN and Midland Railways were uninterested in the line, the company was transferred to and vested in the Great Central Railway as from 1 January 1906, under the terms of the Great Central Railway Act of 4 August 1905.

## CHAPTER XI

# TO THE PRESENT DAY — A SURVEY

Only two short sections of the former St Helens Railway still retain any regular passenger services, as the rest have succumbed to the attacks of buses and private cars. Liverpool-Wigan trains still pass through St Helens over a very short stretch of the local company's line, while the Speke Junction-Ditton Junction section is traversed by the 25kV electric services between Merseyside and London. Only local trains now stop at Ditton station, but passengers can no longer pass from them into the heart of the St Helens Railway.

The lines, which together formed the inverted 'T' of the St Helens Railway system, all converged on Widnes, and this provides a convenient starting point from which to discuss the development and decline of passenger services over the last hundred years. The opening of the deviation line in 1869 improved traffic flows through the town, but with the inauguration of Liverpool-London services over the Runcorn bridge in the same year, Ditton Junction — the suffix was added in the early 1870s, — became the terminus for most trains on the former St Helens Railway system, only the occasional through train keeping alive the original aim of an independent through route between Liverpool and Manchester.

By 1871 trains between St Helens and Widnes had increased to seven in each direction on weekdays with three on Sundays, and within the next thirty years all were extended to terminate at Ditton Junction, with a further increase to nine services on weekdays. Motive power was generally provided by Webb 2-4-2 tanks or 0-6-2 tanks, which were to dominate services over the line for many years. On 1 October 1911, the LNWR introduced a steam railmotor service, and opened halts at Ann Street in Widnes, and at Union Bank Farm, between Farnworth & Bold and Clock Face, while Peasley Cross was reclassified as a railmotor halt from the same date. The use of steam railcars was short-lived, as auto fitted Webb tanks capable of operating four coach trains were soon found more suitable for dealing with the often heavy traffic. The next thirty years, however, saw a gradual decline in patronage and frequency of service, so that by the summer of 1949, the 'Ditton Dodger', as the trains were affectionately known, had been reduced to a basic workman's service with three trains in each direction in the morning and the same at night, leaving a long gap between 8.30 am and 4.15 pm on Mondays to Fridays. Two additional trains in the middle of the day ran on Saturdays, but two evening trains were withdrawn, so the service remained at six trains in each direction. There were no Sunday services, and no concessions for Saturday night entertainment, as the last train over the line completed its journey at 6.37 pm. With such services the proposals for withdrawal came as no surprise, and despite protests from workpeople over the much longer journey times by 'bus, the services were withdrawn from 18 June 1951, the last train over the line on the previous Saturday being the 5.56 pm from St Helens, suitably powered by a Webb 2-4-2 tank.

The St Helens-Rainford Junction line started the twentieth century with the closure of Gerard's Bridge station from 1 August 1904, an early victim of increased road transport competition. But passengers over the branch itself continued to be well served with eight or more trains in each direction on weekdays. The LYR had introduced steam railmotors on its Ormskirk-Rainford Junction line on 1 July 1906, but the LNWR did not follow suit until 1 October 1911, when it opened a new halt at Old Mill Lane between Rookery and Crank. As on the Widnes line, the LNWR soon went over to auto-fitted tank engines for the 'Flying Flea', but on the Ormskirk line the LYR persevered with steam railmotors on the 'Skem Dodger' for a while longer, before it was taken over by Aspinall 2-4-2 tanks. The decline in patronage and services closely followed that on the Widnes line, and Crank became an unstaffed halt from 9 September 1940. Passenger services were ultimately reduced to a morning and evening workman's service of three trains in each direction. Despite local protests the last train left Rainford Junction for St Helens on 16 June 1951, although the passenger service on the LY Ormskirk branch was not finally withdrawn until 5 November 1956.

Services over the Ditton Junction-Widnes-Warrington line, which enjoyed such endearing nicknames as the 'Jam and Herring' or the 'Banana Run', because of their original association with Garston Docks, were never really regarded as anything more than local trains, with the sole exception of the late night Liverpool-York mail train, which ultimately became the last regular passenger train to use the line.

In April 1910, besides the 'Mail', there were ten through workings on weekdays between Liverpool Lime Street and Manchester London Road, but only seven in the reverse direction, plus an extra train on Saturdays. There were a relatively large number of shorter workings, particularly between Manchester and Warrington, and between Widnes and Liverpool, but space precludes a full treatment of these. Sunday services consisted of three through trains in each direction, but with the 'Mail' in the eastbound direction only, and early morning trains from St Helens to Liverpool and from Warrington Arpley to Broadheath.

Although many of the services were worked by Webb 2-4-2 tanks and 0-6-2 tanks, the Widnes-Warrington line had in addition to these a fascinating variety of motive power, as both the LNWR and LMSR put many erstwhile express locomotives into semi-retirement over it. 'Precedent' 2-4-0s and 'Renown' 4-4-0s were followed by 'Precursors' and 'George the Fifths', while Claughton and Experiment 4-6-0s were also found from time to time. Many were blessed with the amazing variety of names that the LNWR distributed at random among its locomotives. *Lazonby, Pitt, The Auditor, Britomart, Resolution, Sultan* and *Flying Fox* are some that have been recorded, but only hint at the multitude which traversed the line. The massive Bowen Cooke 4-6-2 tanks made a fleeting appearance, and 0-6-0 and 0-8-0 tender engines were pressed into service in time of need. In LMS days these were joined by North Staffordshire 0-6-2 tanks, Stanier 2-6-2 tanks and LY 2-4-2 tanks, the latter having a regular working until the 1950s. Gradually the variety decreased, and after the demise of the LNWR locomotives most services were handled by LMS and BR 2-6-2 tanks with three-coach autosets, although from time to time various tender engines were also used.

Withdrawal of the Widnes-St Helens passenger services in 1951 did not greatly affect workings over the Ditton Junction-Warrington line, as connections had generally been poor. There was only one through working between Manchester and Liverpool, the 4.19 pm from London Road, which took 1 hour 40 minutes for the journey. One train from Manchester and one from Warrington went as far as Ditton Junction to complete the sparse westbound service on weekdays only. There were far more trains in the Manchester direction, but the only through service was on Saturdays. The 'Mail' was diverted on Sundays via Earlestown at the beginning of the 1959 winter timetable to avoid the expense of opening signal boxes for just one train. At the end of October 1959, there was a short-lived dieselisation of the local trains, but these reverted to steam haulage early in 1961. By that time there were no less than six terminal points for trains on these services with a high level of light engine or empty stock working. The service was cited for withdrawal, but when this took place from 10 September 1962, only Widnes South was closed to passenger and parcels services, as Warrington Bank Quay Low Level was still kept open to cater for the Liverpool-York train. This was rerouted from 4 January 1965 to run via Allerton Junction and the CLC line to Stockport, and thus the last regular service disappeared from this section of the St Helens Railway, although some excursions and diverted traffic continued to use it.

The last local service to run over any significant section of the former St Helens Railway was that between St Helens Shaw Street and St Helens Junction, with certain trains extended to Earlestown and Warrington, and in earlier days even as far south as Acton Bridge. The bulk of services on what was known as the 'Junction Bus' or 'The Motor' were worked by Webb tanks, until replaced by Ivatt 2-6-2 tanks in the early 1950s. One of these, 41286, remained in use after dieselisation, and deputised on many passenger services as well as its own special working, the 17.10 (FO) Prescot-St Helens Shaw Street, until this was withdrawn in late 1965.

Services on the Liverpool-St Helens Shaw Street-Wigan line were dieselised from 5 January 1959 with a frequency almost doubled on weekdays, but on Sundays an hourly service in the afternoon between Liverpool and St Helens only. Two years later it was estimated that over three times as many passengers were using the services compared with steam days, and as on 2 January 1961 there had been a general introduction of diesel railcars on the Liverpool-Manchester main line, as well as on the line down to St Helens Junction and Warrington, a similar increase was expected on these. Services between town and junction were increased from eight to thirty three, probably the highest in the history of the line, as even in the latter years of the nineteenth century the average had only been about 24 workings in each direction. Nevertheless, despite the general increase in passenger revenue, and the opening of a new station in St Helens in 1961, Sunday services between Liverpool and St Helens were withdrawn for a period from the start of the 1962 winter timetable, and the Beeching Report 'The Re-Shaping of British Railways' recommended the total withdrawal of all passenger services from St Helens — by then a town of over 100,000 inhabitants. Services between St Helens Shaw Street, St Helens Junction and Warrington were withdrawn from 14 June 1965, but the fight to save the Liverpool-St Helens-Wigan service ultimately bore fruit, and it became the recipient of an increasing amount of grant aid from 1969 until 1972, when local services calling at two or more stations between Liverpool and Eccleston Park were integrated in the Merseyside PTE, which was expected to cover an increasing portion of any losses incurred by these trains. During the last few years proposals to electrify the line have formed part of several improvement plans for passenger services on Merseyside, and its future now appears reasonably secure.

*Garston to Warrington*

As we have seen, the Speke Junction-Ditton Junction section of the Garston branch soon gained new importance as part of the Liverpool-London main line, which gave it a significance far removed from the relatively humdrum existence pursued by the rest of the system. In 1864 the Garston branch was linked with Liverpool by the opening of the Garston & Liverpool Railway, but although it was no longer used as a major through route after the inauguration of full express passenger services over the CLC Liverpool-Manchester line in 1874, it gained a service into Liverpool Lime Street over the new curve at Allerton, which had been opened in January of the previous year. This was withdrawn as an economy measure from 15 April 1917 until 5 May

1919, when Garston Dock and Church Road stations were also temporarily closed. Church Road station closed completely on 3 July 1939, and the Liverpool Lime Street-Garston passenger service was discontinued on 16 July 1947.

The Garston Dock complex continued to expand with a third dock — the Stalbridge Dock — being opened in 1909. A considerable and stable trade developed in specialised commodities such as timber, coal and bananas. The latter really started in 1912, when Elder Fyffes transferred their activities from Manchester, but although by the mid 1930s 100,000 tons a year were passing through the port, this traffic ended in 1965 under a re-organisation of the banana trade.

Continual improvements were made in the facilities for coal and timber, and after one major project had been completed in 1936, over 8,000 waggons could be accommodated in the immediate area, giving a capacity in excess of 100,000 tons of mineral traffic, while 85 acres of land were available for timber storage. In 1966 a Freightliner Terminal was opened on the site of the St Helens Railway coal yard adjacent to Garston Dock station, and the facilities there have been continually improved and extended since then. Over a million tons of coal are still exported annually through the docks, but despite this and other traffic in timber and steel, the size of the facilities at the docks have been drastically reduced, as modern handling methods have been introduced. Traditional tipping facilities for unbraked coal waggons continued in operation in the Old and Stalbridge Docks, until those on the latter were taken out of use to facilitate the construction of a new bulk unloading plant at a cost of £1.5 million, which is served by block trains of tippler waggons with coal transported by conveyor to the dockside. This was officially opened on 8 June 1981 and, together with the Freightliner terminal, should guarantee a secure future to the Garston branch, although its link with the CLC lines was severed on 21 August 1977 with the closure of the line from Cressington Junction.

Speke Junction shed has long been closed and demolished with its remaining duties taken over by the new depot at Allerton, opened on 10 July 1960. Three stations between here and Ditton have disappeared — Speke, closed to all traffic from 22 September 1930, Woodside Goods, which closed on 6 March 1961, after having been an unstaffed coal depot since 20 April 1953, and Halebank. This was known in St Helens Railway days and until 1 November 1874 as Halewood, then as Halebank (for Hale) until the end of May 1895, when it became known simply as Halebank. It, too, was closed as a wartime economy measure from 1 January 1917 to 5 May 1919, the final closure being effected from 15 September 1958. Ditton watertroughs are long gone, but the creosote and sleeper works still function. Ditton Junction was completely rebuilt in 1961 prior to electrification of main line services, and reverted to its original name of

Ditton from 3 May 1971.

The original St Helens Railway lines into Widnes were closed from 14 February 1966, and all trains must now use the later goods lines, which ran south of Ditton Junction station, and then burrowed under the LNWR main line to reach the original alignment at Widnes No 8 (West Deviation) Box. South of the main line was the western section of the Hutchinson Dock & Estate railway system, and the West Bank Dock of the St Helens Railway, long since derelict and filled in. Various factories in that area were also served by the GC & Midland Marsh branch, but this was closed in 1964, so that the only significant rail movement in the area now comes from the British Oxygen Company plant officially opened in July 1971 at a cost of £12 million. Company-owned block trains carrying oxygen and nitrogen at low temperature had been operating since the previous December, and over one million tons were safely transported to various BOC depots around the country within five years of the opening.

The railway geography of Widnes centred on the flat almost right-angled crossing of the original St Helens line of 1833 and the Garston-Warrington, which despite various connections and the opening of the deviation line, continued to pose operating problems, further complicated by the level crossing across Victoria Road. The LNW station on the deviation was renamed Widnes South on 5 January 1959 and, after its closure to passengers from 10 September 1962, continued to be used for Rugby League specials until its demolition in 1965. It became an unstaffed coal depot from 18 January of the same year and was closed completely, apart from private sidings traffic, from 31 March 1969.

Passenger services on the GC & Midland loop line, which ran very close to the north on a viaduct at this point, were withdrawn from 5 October 1964, since when much of its course has been obliterated in new road works, although the small section at Tanhouse Lane still performs a useful function. The so called Landowners Branch, which left the loop line at Moor Lane Junction to serve Broughton Copper Works, was closed on 1 June 1953, as was the line to the Liver Alkali Works.

The six-road locomotive shed at Widnes, which closed in April 1964, was situated between the deviation line and the connection to the St Helens line. It was essentially for freight engines, although even as late as 1950 it had a few Stainier 2-6-2 tanks, which were used on passenger trains as well as for trip working and shunting. Its allocation during the last fifteen years of its existence remained fairly constant at 20-30 locomotives, with Stanier 2-8-0s as the main heavy motive power after the demise of the LNWR 0-8-0s. A wide variety of types covered the lighter duties, and steam working continued into the early months of 1968, since when, apart from class 08 shunters, the most common

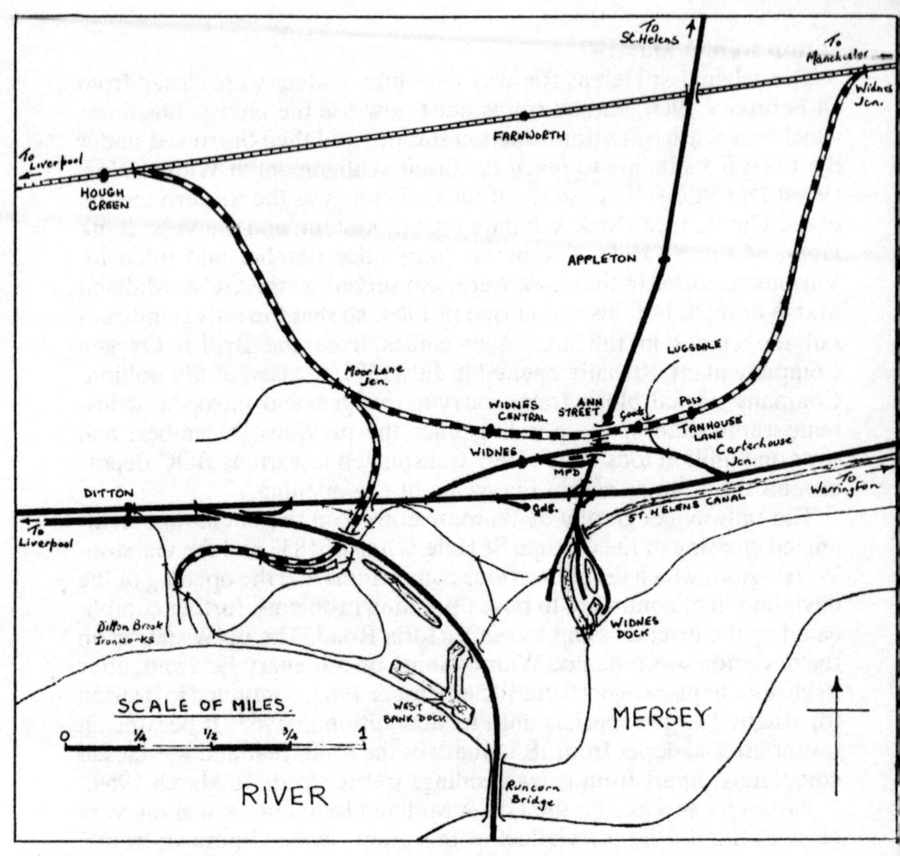


WIDNES AT THE TIME OF THE GROUPING – 1922

LONDON & NORTH WESTERN RAILWAY
CHESHIRE LINES COMMITTEE
GREAT CENTRAL & MIDLAND JOINT COMMITTEE
INDUSTRIAL LINES (PRIVATE & RAILWAY-OWNED)

diesel types to be found in both Widnes and Garston have been Classes 25, 37, 40 and 47, with a growing number of Class 56 locomotives in the last few years.

The deviation line continues on its embankment to join the original Widnes-Warrington line at Carterhouse Junction, near which the spur from the LNWR Lugsdale goods depot, closed on 1 April 1966, trailed in from the north after passing under the GC & Midland loop.

The original Garston-Warrington line continued on the level from Widnes No 8 Box past the connection to the Hutchinson Dock lines and the LNW Hutchinson Street coal depot, which closed on 2

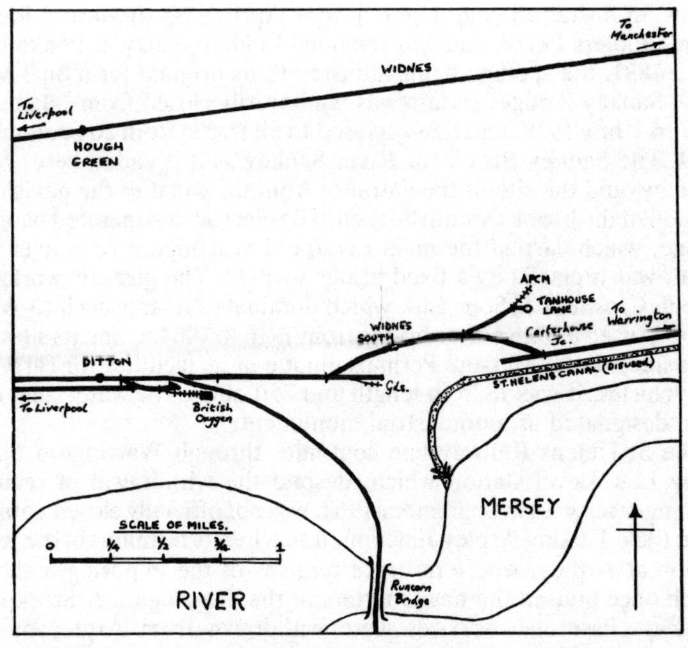


WIDNES IN 1982.

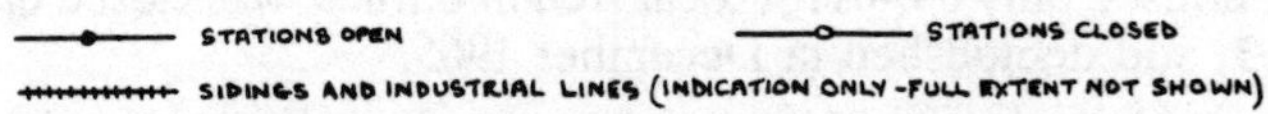


December 1968, apart from private siding traffic. Close to Widnes No 6 box, and adjacent to Victoria Road, was the site of the second St Helens Railway station, some distance west of the flat crossing with the St Helens line. By 1968 one track was used for waggon storage and now, apart from a short section from Carterhouse Junction retained mainly to serve a stone terminal, all the lines in this area have now been lifted.

After Carterhouse Junction the Warrington line runs on a more or less level course along the northern bank of the canal almost all the way to Sankey Bridges. The main landmark is now the coal-fired power station at Fidlers Ferry, which is served by merry-go-round trains from collieries in Lancashire, North Wales and Yorkshire, and should guarantee a long life for this section of the St Helens Railway system. The old canal entrance to the Mersey can still be seen, but little trace now remains of Fidlers Ferry & Penketh station, closed to passengers on 2 January 1950, and to freight on 2 December 1963, after functioning as an unstaffed coal depot since 4 April 1960. It started life as simply Fidlers Ferry, and was renamed Fiddlers Ferry & Penketh in April 1881, the spelling being adjusted to its original form on 3 May 1920. Sankey Bridges station was temporarily closed from 1 January 1917 to 1 July 1919, and finally closed to all traffic from 26 September 1949. The Sankey Brook (or River Sankey as it is called here) runs close by, and the site of the entrance from the canal to the navigable portion of the brook can still be seen. The electrically operated bascule bridge, which carried the main Liverpool-Warrington road over the canal, was replaced by a fixed bridge in 1972. The gigantic works of Joseph Crosfield & Sons Ltd, which dominate the approach to Warrington, used a transporter bridge from 1916 to 1964 to link its sites on both sides of the Mersey. Perhaps unique in its facilities for carrying rail vehicles, it was 187ft in length and 75ft above the water, and has been designated as an industrial monument.

The St Helens Railway line continues through Warrington Bank Quay Low Level station which, despite the withdrawal of regular passenger services in September 1962, was not officially closed until 14 June 1965. Passing Arpley Junction, it reaches its terminus in the joint station at Arpley, where no trace remains of the imposing building which once housed the headquarters of the Warrington & Stockport Railway. Passenger services were withdrawn from Arpley on 15 September 1958, despite its closeness to the town centre, and it closed to freight traffic on 9 August 1965, apart from private siding traffic. The two-road locomotive shed, which after the end of passenger services, housed only 0-6-0s for local freight dutues, was closed on 19 May 1963, and demolished in December 1965.

*Northwards to St Helens*

Back at Widnes, we renew our acquaintance with the St Helens Canal, which before it succumbed to the ravages of time, could look back on two centuries of service to the community. Traffic in the latter half of the nineteenth century was still heavy, and even as late as 1888 over 500,000 tons of cargo were carried each year. But coal soon vanished from the waterway and by the turn of the century it was dependent on the various minerals, sands and chemicals bound for St Helens, together with sugar, which was destined to be its last major cargo. Although in 1905 a mere 292,985 tons were carried, only the last half mile of the Ravenhead branch had been closed in 1898. Very few boats passed up to St Helens in the first two decades of the twentieth century, but no major closures took place until 1931, when five miles of the canal north of Newton Common Lock were abandoned, although the channel was retained as a feeder and for industrial purposes.

Although traffic fell to 94,016 tons in 1939 and a mere 20,638 tons in 1946, flats continued to work up to the Sankey Sugar Company's wharf, just south of the L & M Sankey viaduct. But in 1959 bulk transport of raw sugar was transferred to road, and all traffic soon ceased, although the waterway was not formally abandoned until the British Waterways Act of 1963. Some stretches in St Helens were filled in, but a more ambitious scheme was started in 1972 to fill in about seven miles of the waterway south of St Helens because of the danger of flooding. Nevertheless interesting relics still remain, and a walk along the still watered stretches in St Helens and Widnes gives some idea of the industries it once served.

The original St Helens Railway line of 1833 started from its dock adjacent to the canal locks, and the whole area, which was once covered by sidings and John Hutchinson's No 1 Works, is now being reclaimed and landscaped to highlight some of the relics of its industrial past. The line from Widnes No 4 Dock Juncion to Widnes Canal Bridge was officially taken out of use on 4 November 1968, with the line from Widnes No 4 to Widnes West Deviation Junction following in March 1969. The remains of the turning mechanism for the swivel bridge over the canal, built by the Haigh Foundry of Wigan in 1832, were still in position in the early 1970s, but no trace remained of the original Runcorn Gap station.

The St Helens line was joined at Widnes No 2 Box, just south of Ann Street Halt, by the connection from No 7 Box on the deviation line. After many years as a useful freight line and diversionary route, it has now been almost completely closed, although its decline really began some 15 years ago when the section between Widnes No 7 and St Helens Junction was reduced to goods line status at the beginning of December 1967. Further reductions were made on 14 December 1969, when the section between Farnworth & Bold and Sutton Oak Junction was singled and worked under the electric token block system. The end came when the line between Widnes No 7 and St Helens Junction was closed as a through route from 1 November 1981. Two sections — from Sutton Oak to Sutton Manor Colliery, and from Widnes No 1 to Farnworth & Bold — were retained as single lines, the latter only temporarily.

A major development in the railway layout at Widnes was made on 16 March 1961, when a single track chord line was opened from Widnes No 1 on the St Helens line to Tanhouse Lane on the GC & Midland loop. This was the first direct connection between the two systems in the area, and was opened for two reasons, firstly to facilitate transfer of engines for shunting duties, and secondly to enable the anhydrite trains from Long Meg sidings on the Settle and Carlisle line to gain access to the United Sulphuric Acid Company plant adjacent to Tanhouse Lane. In April 1964, a thrice-weekly 1,000 ton block train from Snodland in Kent to the Cement Manufacturing Company depot at Tanhouse Lane was introduced to supplement existing trains from

Caldon, near Leek, and it is this traffic coupled with some waggon repair that still keeps alive this last section of the loop line, as the 'Long Megs' came to an end in 1972. In fact a new connection from Tanhouse Lane to the deviation line near Carterhouse Junction was built to facilitate the closure of the greater part of the line to St Helens. This connection was brought into use on 18 April 1982, and the section of line between Widnes No 7 and Farnworth & Bold was officially taken out of use, although track lifting north of Appleton had begun well before that date.

The St Helens line began its long steady climb out of Widnes through a dreary industrial environment past the sites of Ann Street Halt and Appleton, which were both closed on 18 June 1951. In steam days the gradient, which soon stiffened to 1 in 70, meant that heavy freights often needed assistance from the 'Vine Banker' up to Farnworth & Bold, where factory sidings were still in use until the closure of this section of line. The station, just north of where the St Helens line crossed high above the deep cutting containing the CLC Liverpool-Manchester line, was known simply as Farnworth until 2 January 1890. It too lost its passenger services on 18 June 1951, and was closed to freight traffic except for private sidings from 1 June 1964.

After passing the site of Union Bank Halt, the line came to the triangular junction to Sutton Manor Colliery which is still active, but from which, in bygone days, a line ran across the L & M main line to reach Lea Green Colliery, which ceased production in August 1964. Another triangular junction once led off to Clock Face colliery, but railborne traffic had ceased well before its closure in March 1966. In 1845 there were 363 collieries in the Lancashire coalfield against only eleven in 1966. Now only two, Sutton Manor and Bold, remain in the St Helens area, but at the time of writing their future appears reasonably secure, as additional funds have recently been made available for development.

Just north of Clock Face, which functioned as an unstaffed halt from 12 July 1926 until its closure, extensive sidings on both sides of the line, which were used to marshal coal traffic and gave access to the former St Helens Railway locomotive works, were finally closed about 1967. The works were in use as a sheeting works and general stores from 1872 until the 1960s, since when the site has been given over to industrial use including a car crushing plant with rail access from the L & M line.

As the L & M line is crossed the layout at St Helens Junction, as well as Bold Power Station and Bold Colliery can be clearly seen. Freight traffic was withdrawn from St Helens Junction from 6 January 1964, and the former passenger lines, which dived under the St Helens line before joining it on the west side near Sutton Oak Junction, were taken out of use on 2 March 1969. It was on this section that the short lived

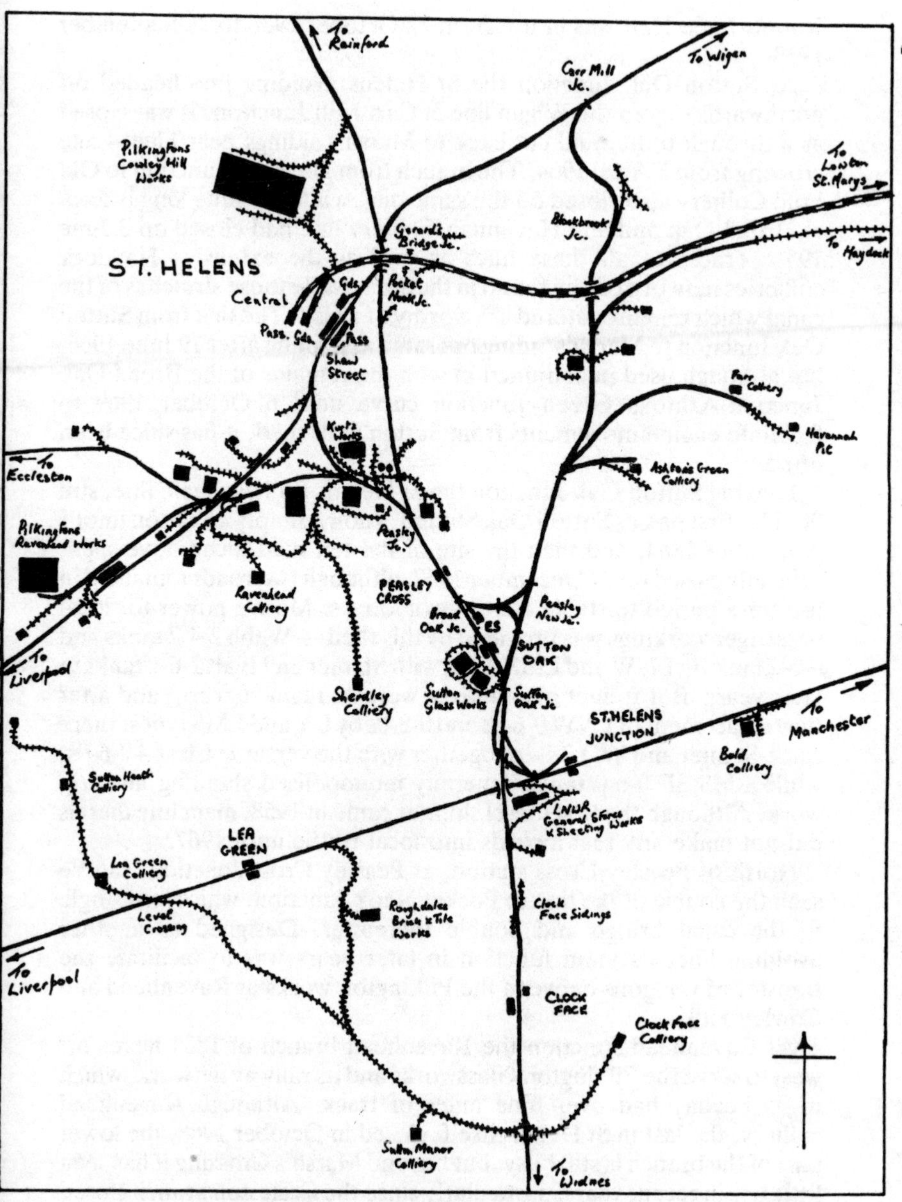


ST. HELENS AT THE GROUPING – 1922.

LONDON & NORTH WESTERN RAILWAY – PRINCIPAL LINES
GREAT CENTRAL RAILWAY – PRINCIPAL LINES
INDUSTRIAL LINES – PRIVATE AND RAILWAY-OWNED

Robins Lane Halt was in use from 12 October 1936 to 26 September 1938.

At Sutton Oak Junction the St Helens avoiding line headed off northwards to join the Wigan line at Carr Mill Junction. It was closed as a through route, and cut back to Marsh's sidings near Fleet Lane crossing from 6 April 1964. The branch from Haydock Junction to Old Fold Colliery also closed on the same day, while the mile long branch to Broad Oak and and Havannah Colliery line had closed on 3 June 1951. Traces of all these lines as well as the extensive Haydock collieries network can be found in the area, while those stretches of the canal which remain watered are worthy of a visit. The line from Sutton Oak Junction to Marsh's Siding operated as a siding after 19 June 1966, but although used in conjunction with the remains of the Broad Oak Junction-Ashtons Green Junction curve until 6 October 1969 to facilitate engine movements from Sutton Oak shed, it has since been lifted.

Leaving Sutton Oak Junction the St Helens Railway main line, still double, first passes Sutton Oak Station, known simply as Sutton until 1 November 1864, and then the site of the ten road locomotive shed, officially closed on 27 December 1967, although two roads remained in use for a period to stable diesel locomotives. Motive power for local passenger workings was provided by this shed — Webb 2-4-2 tanks and 0-6-2 tanks in LNW and LMS days, with Stanier and Ivatt 2-6-2 tanks in later years. But freight locomotives were its main concern, and after the replacement of LNW 0-6-0s and 0-8-0s by LY and LMS types, there came Stanier and WD 2-8-0s together with the versatile Class 4 2-6-0s, while LMS 3F 0-6-0 tanks generally monopolised shunting and trip work. Although the first diesel shunter came in 1958, main line diesels did not make any real inroads into local traffic until 1967.

North of Peasley Cross station, at Peasley Cross Junction, can be seen the course of the line to Pocket Nook Junction, which was single to the canal bridge and double thereafter. Designed as another avoiding line, its main function in later years was to facilitate the transfer of waggons between the Pilkington works at Ravenhead and Cowley Hill.

At Ravenhead Junction the Ravenhead branch of 1834 heads off west to serve the Pilkington Glassworks and its railway network, which in its heyday had over nine miles of track. Although Ravenhead colliery, the last in St Helens itself, closed in October 1968, the lower part of the branch is still busy, but beyond Marsh's Crossing it has seen little use in recent years, particularly since the Eccleston branch closed on 10 October 1967, and the fortunes of the factories it served have declined.

The St Helens Railway main line continues from Ravenhead Junction to be joined by the line from Huyton just short of St Helens No 1

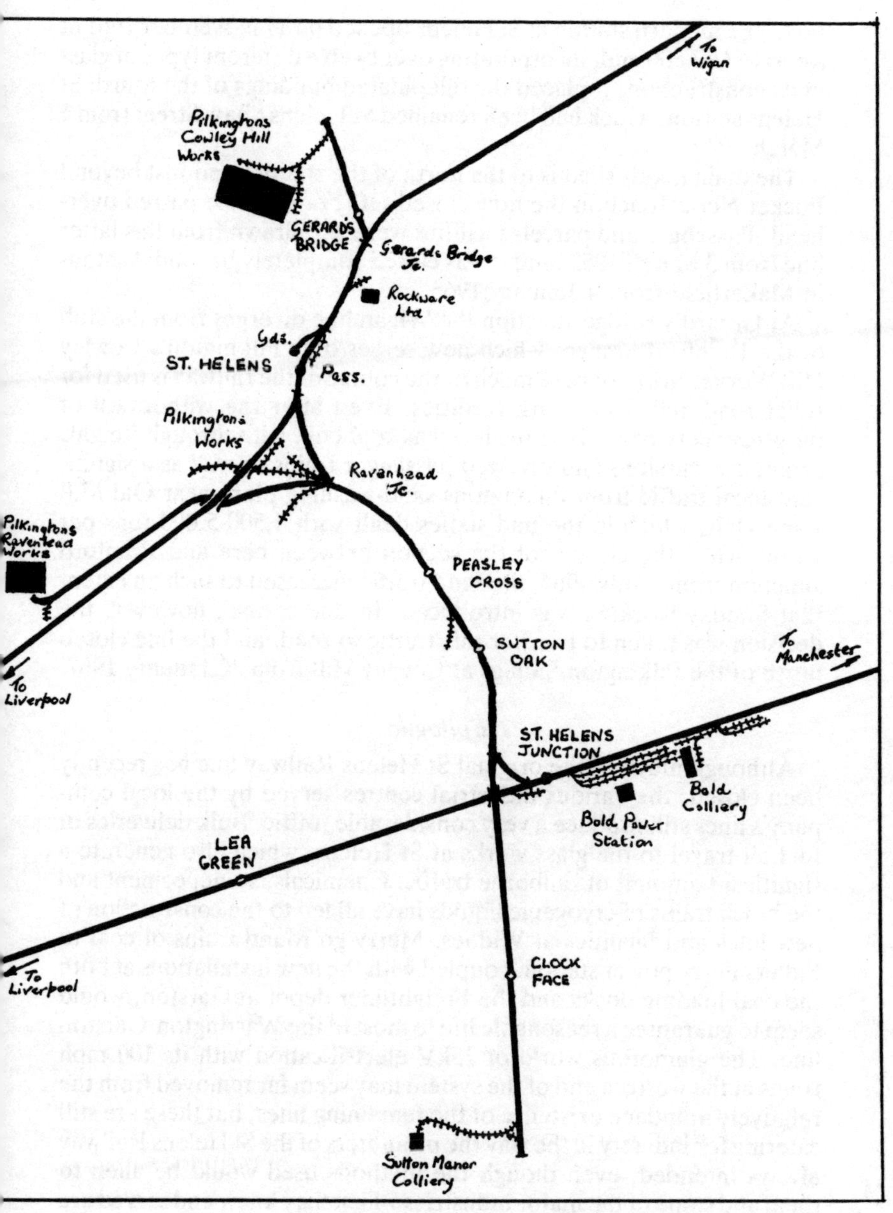


ST. HELENS IN 1982.

STATIONS OPEN — STATIONS CLOSED

SIDINGS AND INDUSTRIAL LINES (INDICATION ONLY - FULL EXTENT NOT SHOWN)

box. The modern station at St Helens opened on 17 November 1961 at a cost of £80,000 and, incorporating over twelve different types of glass in its construction, replaced the dilapidated buildings of the fourth St Helens station, which had been renamed St Helens Shaw Street from 1 March 1949.

The main goods shed is to the north of the station, and just beyond Pocket Nook Junction the now closed GC branch once passed overhead. Passenger and parcels facilities were withdrawn from this latter line from 3 March 1952, and it was closed completely beyond Ashton-in-Makerfield from 4 January 1965.

At Gerard's Bridge Junction the Wigan line diverges from the stub of the Rainford branch, which now serves only Pilkington's Cowley Hill Works. North of here much of the course of the railway is used for relief road and linear park facilities. Even after the withdrawal of passenger services in 1951 the line was kept busy with through freight, summer excursions and diverted passenger trains as well as a significant local traffic from Pilkingtons sand-washing plant near Old Mill Lane Halt, which in the mid sixties dealt with 4,500-5,000 tons per week. After the closure of the section between here and Rainford Junction from 6 July 1964, the sand traffic increased to such an extent that Sunday working was introduced. In due course, however, the decision was taken to transfer this traffic to road, and the line closed north of the Pilkington Sidings at Cowley Hill from 30 January 1967.

## *Epilogue*

Although much of the original St Helens Railway line has recently been closed, the various industrial centres served by the local company's lines still produce a very considerable traffic. Bulk deliveries of fuel oil travel to the glass works at St Helens, which also generate a significant amount of railborne traffic. Chemicals, stone, cement and the block trains of cryogenic liquids have all led to the construction of new lines and facilities at Widnes. Merry-go-round trains of coal to Fidlers Ferry power station, coupled with the new installations at both the coal loading docks and the Freightliner depot at Garston, would seem to guarantee a reasonable life to most of the Warrington-Garston line. The glamorous world of 25kV electrification with its 100 mph trains at the western end of the system may seem far removed from the relatively mundane existence of the remaining lines, but these are still catering for industry in the way the promoters of the St Helens Railway always intended, even though the methods used would be alien to them and some of the major industries which they knew and served are now no more than memories.

*Printed by Bookmag, Henderson Road, Inverness*